ILKESTON TO CHESTERFIELD

including many collieries

Vic Mitchell and Keith Smith

MP Middleton Press

Published February 2019
First reprint July 2020

ISBN 978 1 910356 26 5

© Middleton Press, 2019

Production Editor & Cover design Deborah Esher
Typesetting & Design Cassandra Morgan

Published by
    Middleton Press
    Easebourne Lane
    Midhurst
    West Sussex
    GU29 9AZ
Tel: 01730 813169
Email: info@middletonpress.co.uk
www.middletonpress.co.uk

Printed and bound by CPI Group (UK) Ltd, Croydon, CR0 4YY

INDEX

ACKNOWLEDGEMENTS

We are very grateful for the assistance received from many of those mentioned in the credits, also from R.S.Carpenter, A.J.Castledine, G.Croughton, G.Gartside, J.Hinson (Signalling Record Society), C.M.Howard, N.Langridge, B.Lewis, D. and Dr S. Salter, T.Walsh and, in particular, our always supportive families.

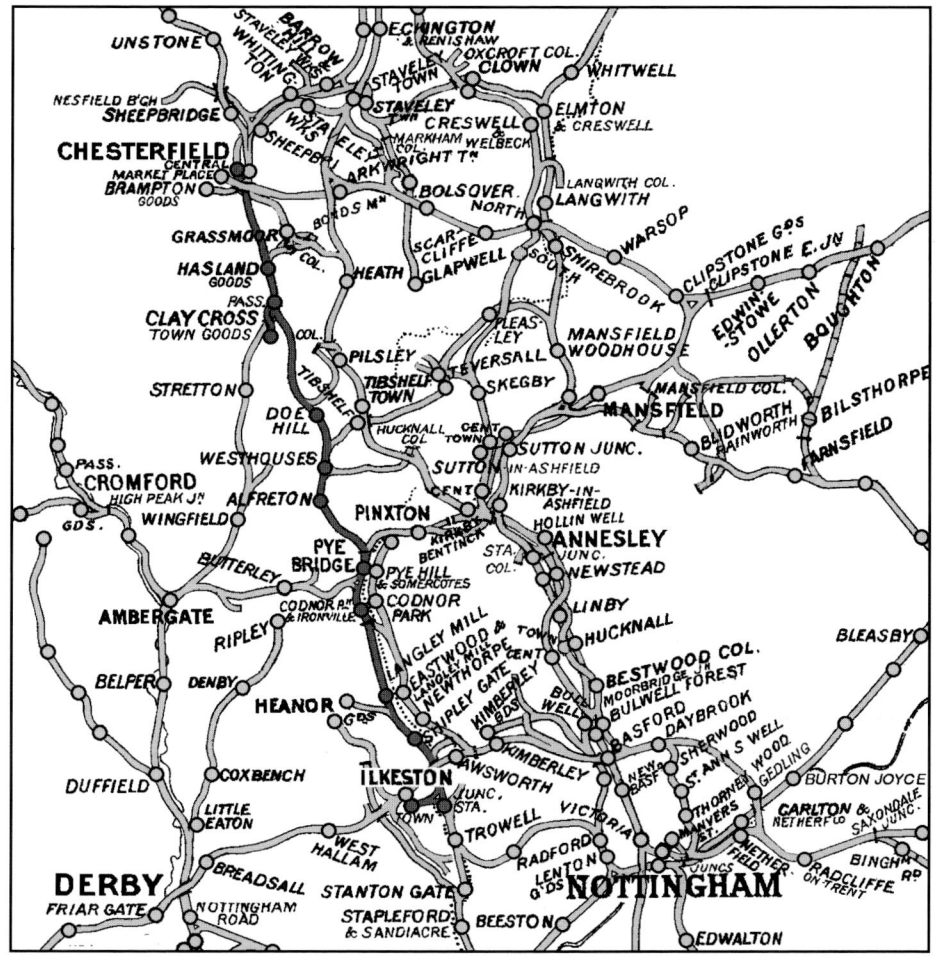

I. The bold line shows our route on this Railway Clearing House map from 1947.

GEOGRAPHICAL SETTING

From Ilkeston northwards, the route runs close to the River Erewash and the Cromford Canal. At Pye Hill, it leaves both and climbs through Alfreton Tunnel. Beyond the summit north of Doe Hill it descends into the valley of the River Rother. The route is in the county of Derbyshire.

Our journey is over coal deposits of different depths. The maps are to the scale of 25ins to 1 mile, with north at the top, unless otherwise indicated.

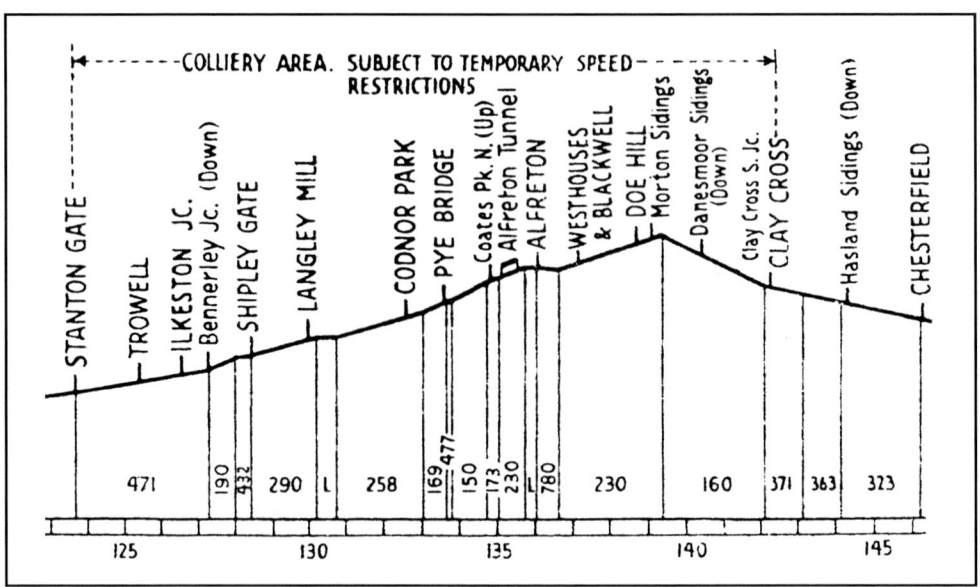

HISTORICAL BACKGROUND

The main line from Leicester through Loughborough was that of the Midland Counties Railway. It ran north to Trent Junction and opened in 1840. This was roughly halfway between Derby and Nottingham on the MCR's earliest line, which had come into use in 1839. The MCR became part of the Midland Railway in May 1844.

The route north to Codnor Park was opened by the MR on 6th September 1847. From Codnor Park, the line was extended along the Erewash Valley through Pye Bridge to Mansfield on 9th October 1849. The main line from Pye Bridge to Clay Cross was opened for freight on 1st November 1861, and for passengers on 1st May 1862.

At Clay Cross, our route met the NMR's Ambergate to Leeds route, which had opened in 1840. The Ilkeston Town branch carried passengers from 6th September 1847 to 16th June 1947, but not in 1870-76. The line north from Chesterfield to Dore and Sheffield was opened by the MR in 1870.

The MR became a large part of the London Midland & Scottish Railway in 1923 and this was a major constituent of the London Midland Region of British Railways under the Nationalisation scheme, in 1948.

Following privatisation, the bulk of the route was operated by Central Trains. This operator commenced running on 2nd March 1997 and continued to do so until 10th November 2007. Under its Citylink long-distance brand, Norwich to Liverpool via Nottingham services operated on this route between Trowell Junction and Chesterfield, at an hourly frequency. Midland Mainline was the operator of principal long-distance services between London St. Pancras, Leicester, Nottingham, Derby and Sheffield between 28th April 1996 and 10th November 2007. It routed some of its morning and evening peak services between London St Pancras and Sheffield via this route, thus avoiding Derby.

Both Central Trains (in this area) and Midland Mainline became part of the new East Midlands Trains franchise on 11th November 2007. From December 2008, Northern also began operating an hourly Nottingham to Leeds service, between Trowell Junction and Chesterfield on this route. This franchise ran until 31st March 2016, when it was replaced by another of the same name the following day.

PASSENGER SERVICES

The train frequency in the early years was irregular, but the service improved and then declined, as the examples reveal. The number of through trains gradually increased.

	Fast		Slow	
	Weekdays	Sundays	Weekdays	Sundays
1870	-	-	6	4
1890	4	0	10	3
1910	5	0	13	3
1946	1	2	9	2
1960	0	0	9	0

Local services ceased in 1967. With the reopening of Alfreton, plus the suffix '& Mansfield Parkway', on 7th May 1973, a service of eight weekday trains, with three on Sundays, arrived. A new station for Ilkeston came on 2nd April 2017, with a good daily service.

December 1870

NOTTINGHAM, ILKESTON, PYE BRIDGE, AMBERGATE, and CHESTERFIELD.—Midland.

Week Days.

Miles	Station																								
		mrn	mrn	mrn	mrn	mrn	mrn	mrn	mrn	mrn	mrn	mrn	aft	aft	aft	aft	mrn	mrn	aft	aft	aft	aft	aft	aft	aft
	606 London (St. Pan) dep	....	....	2 25	....	4 25	4 25	....	4 25	....	9 0	9 0	9 0	....	....	10 25	11 0	11 0	11 0	....	12 25	1 50	1 50	....	4 33
	665 Derby n	....	....	....	....	....	....	....	....	10 10	....	....	10 33	....	....	....	12 19	....	....	....	....	3 35	....	....	....
—	Nottingham ...... dep	5 35	6 12	6 15	6 43	7 18	7 50	8 28	8 25	9 0	9 12	9 42	10 10	11 20	12 25	12 25	12 45	1 21	1 37	1 40	2 30	2 40	2 53	3 04	4 10	4 17	4 30	5 15
3¾	Beeston	5 42	6 20	....	6 51	7 26	7 58	....	8 33	....	9 20	9 50	10 18	11 33	12 32	12 33	12 53	....	....	....	2 48	....	3 38	....	....	....	5 23
4¼	Attenborough	5 47	6 24	....	....	7 30	8 2	....	....	9 24	....	....	11 37	....	....	12 58	1 4	....	....	....	2 52	....	....	....	....	....	5 27
6¼	Trent 617, 671 { arr	6 20	....	7 35	....	8 38	....	....	9 30	....	....	....	11 22	....	....	1 19	....	....	2 4	....	....	....	....	....	....	5 32
	{ dep	6 24	....	7 46	....	8 43	....	....	9 41	....	....	....	11 47	....	12 44	1 21	....	....	2 7	....	....	....	....	....	....	5 38
7¾	Long Eaton	5 56	6 39	....	7 0	7 49	8 16	....	8 47	....	9 31	10 5	10 51	11 45	12 22	12 49	12 42	1 21	7 1	1 34	....	3 0	3 39	4 4	4 17	....	5 43
9¼	Stapleford and Sandiacre	6 1	6 45	....	7 6	7 55	8 19	....	8 53	....	9 36	10 10	10 57	11 51	12 28	12 42	12 42	12 42	1 59	....	3 6	4 10	4 24	....	....	5 49
10⅞	Stanton Gate	6 49	....	7 10	7 59	8 23	....	8 57	....	9 43	....	11 0	11 55	12 32	12 52	....	....	....	3 10	....	4 13	4 28	....	....	....	5 53
12	Trowell ....[Cossall	6 54	6 33	7 16	....	8 29	8 45	9 3	9 0	9 49	....	....	12 0	....	1 24	....	....	2 17	....	....	4 18	4 36	....	....	....	5 59
13½	Ilkeston Junction and	7 0	6 39	7 21	....	8 35	8 50	9 9	9 0	9 55	....	....	12 5	12 42	....	1 29	....	2 13	2 50	3 21	3 49	4 40	....	4 51	....	6 2
14	Ilkeston Town { arr	7 5	6 43	7 25	....	8 38	8 53	9 12	9 0	10 0	....	....	12 10	....	1 32	....	....	2 17	....	3 24	3 52	4 44	....	4 54	....	6 7
	{ dep	6 52	....	7 16	....	8 43	....	8 57	9 46	....	....	12 20	....	2 42	....	....	....	....	....	....	....	....	5 0	....	....
15¼	Shipley Gate	7 3	....	....	....	10 1	....	....	....	12 23	....	....	2 37	....	....	....	....	....	....	....	....	5 8	....	....
16½	Langley Mill and East- [wood	7 14	....	7 30	....	8 53	....	....	10 1	....	....	12 31	....	1 44	....	....	2 58	....	....	....	....	5 14	....	....
19	Codnor Park ★	7 21	....	7 37	....	9 0	....	....	10 16	....	....	12 37	....	1 55	....	3 7	....	....	....	....	....	5 21	....	....
20½	Pye Bridge 637 { arr	7 24	....	7 40	....	9 3	....	....	10 10	....	....	12 40	....	2 1	....	3 10	....	....	....	....	....	5 25	....	....
23⅛	Butterley { [634	7 53	....	....	....	10 54	....	....	....	....	2 19	....	2 19	4 24	....	....	....	....	....	....	....	....
26¾	Ambergate 617 arr	8 0	....	....	....	11 2	....	....	....	....	2 27	....	2 27	4 34	....	....	....	....	....	....	....	....
—	Pye Bridge	dep	7 25	....	9 6	....	....	....	12 4	....	....	12 48	....	2 5	....	3 11	....	....	....	....	....	5 12	5 26	....
22¾	Alfreton † .... [well 687	7 34	....	9 14	....	....	10 27	....	12 48	....	....	3 19	....	....	....	....	....	5 19	5 33	....
24	Westhouses and Black-	7 40	....	9 17	....	10 32	....	12 53	....	....	3 24	....	....	....	....	....	5 24	5 37	....
25¾	Doe Hill	7 46	....	9 22	....	10 37	....	12 58	....	....	3 29	....	....	....	....	....	5 29	5 42	....
29	Clay Cross ‡ 616	7 56	....	9 31	....	10 46	....	1 7	....	....	3 38	....	....	....	....	....	5 39	5 51	....
33	Chesterfield § 607 .. arr	8 2	....	9 38	....	9 57	10 53	....	1 15	....	....	3 48	....	....	....	....	....	5 45	5 47	5 58	....
45½	607 Sheffield .... arr	9 2	....	10 26	....	10 26	10 32	....	1 50	....	....	2 53	4 20	....	....	....	....	5 16	6 23	6 46	....

Week Days—Continued.

Miles	Station	aft	aft	aft	aft	aft	aft	aft	aft	aft	aft	aft	aft	mrn	mrn	aft
	606 London (St. Pan) dep	3 30	3 30	3 30	....	5 0	6 15	6 15	....	....	....	....	12 0	10 50	1 35
	665 Denby n	....	....	5 47	....	....	7 26	....	....	....	....	9 31	....	....
	Nottingham ....dep	5 45	5 56	6 10	6 20	7 20	7 35	7 45	8 0	9 0	10 16	10 42	11 0	....	5 55	9 30	1 30
	Beeston	6 13	....	6 28	....	7 53	8 43	9 8	9 18	10 18	10 38	10 50	11 8	....	6 59	9 38	1 40
	Attenborough	6 32	....	7 57	....	9 12	....	10 43	10 55	11 12	....	9 9	9 43	....
	Trent 617, 671 { arr	6 37	....	8 2	....	....	9 48	4 46	5 31	....
	{ dep	6 44	....	8 28	....	....	10 4	4 56	6 0	....
	Long Eaton	6 2	6 24	6 48	7 19	....	8 57	9 19	10 27	10 28	10 51	11 12	11 20	....	6 17	10 39	6 10
	Stapleford and Sandiacre	6 8	6 31	6 53	7 55	....	9 3	9 25	10 33	10 36	11 6	11 18	11 37	....	6 25	10 14	6 15
	Stanton Gate	6 13	....	6 59	7 59	....	9 7	9 29	10 37	10 41	11 21	11 41	....	6 29	10 19	6 14
	Trowell ....[Cossall	6 19	....	6 44	6 27	7 51	....	9 13	9 35	10 43	10 47	11 13	11 8	11 37	....	6 35	10 25	6 20
	Ilkeston Junction &	6 24	....	6 50	6 33	8 0	....	9 18	9 40	10 51	11 55	11 20	11 29	11 48	....	6 41	10 30	6 25
	Ilkeston Town { arr	6 59	....	7 0	6 39	8 17	....	9 23	9 43	10 55	11 20	11 29	11 48	....	....	....
	{ dep	6 15	....	8 0	....	9 50	10 59	11 3	....	11 53	....	....
	Shipley Gate	6 39	....	....	....	....	....	....	....	....	....
	Langley Mill and East-	6 45	....	8 19	....	9 27	9 11	11 14	....	12 3	....	6 52	10 41	6 34
	Codnor Park ★	6 52	....	8 26	....	9 33	....	....	....	....	....
	Pye Bridge 637 { arr	6 57	....	8 30	....	9 27	11 17	11 26	....	12 11	....	7 5	10 55	6 40
	Butterley { [634	7 19	....	....	....	....	....	....	....	....	....
	Ambergate 617 arr	7 30	....	....	....	....	....	....	....	....	....
	Pye Bridge	dep	6 58	....	8 31	....	9 39	....	....	12 12	....	7 6	....	6 45
	Alfreton † ...[well 637	7 4	....	8 37	....	9 45	....	....	12 17	....	7 15	....	6 53
	Westhouses and Black-	7 9	....	8 42	....	9 50	....	....	....	....	7 21	....	6 58
	Doe Hill	7 14	....	8 47	....	....	....	....	....	....	7 27	....	7 4
	Clay Cross ‡ 616	7 23	....	8 56	....	10 4	....	....	....	....	7 37	....	7 13
	Chesterfield § 607 arr	6 44	7 32	8 9	8 9	9 0	10 11	....	....	....	7 45	2 45	7 20	....
	607 Sheffield .... arr	7 5	8 18	8 30	9 33	11 17	....	....	8 50	3 13	7 55	....

June 1922

NOTES.

B Arrives Sheffield at 11 10 aft on Saturdays.

g Passengers not booked from Derby to these Stations.

K Passengers for Long Eaton and Stations beyond travel via Beeston.

s Stops on Saturdays only.

S Saturday night.

★ Codnor Park and Ironville.

† Alfreton and South Normanton.

‡ Station for North Wingfield (⅜ mile).

§ About ¼ mile to G. C. Main Line Station and over ½ mile to G. C. Market Place Station.

NOTTINGHAM, ILKESTON, PYE BRIDGE, AMBERGATE, and CHESTERFIELD.

December 1938

Week Days.

Miles	Station	mrn	mrn	mrn	mrn	mrn	mrn	mrn	mrn	mrn	mrn	mrn	aft	aft	aft	mrn	aft	mrn	aft	aft	aft	aft	aft	aft
	642 London (St. Pan.) dep	12 5	....	....	....	2 25	....	....	4 25	4 25	....	9 55	....	....	10 30	....	10 55	....	....	....	12 4	1 0	2 10
—	Nottingham ....dep	5 35	6 2	6 13	6 45	7 18	7 25	7 40	7 58	8 30	8 33	9 0	9 10	9 17	9 35	9 50	11 2	11 37	11 48	12 2	12 24	12 47	1 10	1 35	1 48	2 36	2 33	2 43	3 28	3 42	4 13	4 17
3¾	Beeston	5 43	....	6 20	6 52	....	7 32	....	8 6	....	8 40	....	9 17	....	9 42	....	11 44	....	12 9	12 31	12 54	1 17	1 43	....	2 40	2 50	....	3 49	4 21
4¼	Attenborough	....	6 24	....	....	7 29	....	....	8 11	....	9 21	....	9 49	....	11 48	....	12 35	12 58	1 21	....	2 54	....	3 53
6¼	Trent 649 { arr	6 28	....	7 33	....	8 46	....	....	10 1	....	12 15	....	1 25	....	2 46	....	4 8
	{ dep	6 35	....	7 48	....	8 49	....	....	10 5	....	12 25	....	1 39	....	2 51	....	4 22
7¾	Long Eaton	5 58	....	6 41	7 0	7 32	....	8 19	....	8 51	....	9 28	9 50	10 9	....	11 55	12 0	12 25	12 42	12 45	1 34	1 52	....	2 55	3 1	3 42	4 6	4 29
9¼	Stapleford and Sandiacre	6 2	....	6 46	7 5	7 56	....	8 24	....	8 58	....	9 33	9 54	10 14	....	12 0	12 6	12 33	12 47	1 1	1 39	1 57	....	3 0	3 47	4 14	4 38
10⅞	Stanton Gate	....	6 50	7 9	....	....	9 0	....	9 37	....	10 17	....	12 4	12 8	12 55	1 18	....	3 10	....	4 18
12	Trowell ....[Cossall	6 16	6 54	7 13	....	8 2	8 44	....	9 4	....	9 45	....	10 23	....	12 5	12 55	1 18	....	3 15	....	4 42
13½	Ilkeston Junction & arr	6 23	6 58	6 55	7 17	....	7 55	8 36	8 47	9 0	9 10	9 14	....	9 45	9 33	....	12 11	....	12 41	1 6	....	2 9	....	3 18	3 53	4 45
14	Ilkeston Town ¶ { arr	6 23	7 23	7 23	....	7 55	8 39	9 13	9 0	9 13	9 36	....	12 15	12 47	1 32	1 5	2 12	....	2 53	3 21	3 57	5 1
	{ dep	6 3	7 11	....	7 41	8 44	....	8 58	9 40	....	12 21	....	1 32	....	2 42	....	5 6
15¼	Shipley Gate	7 3	....	....	....	....	....	9 40	....	12 25	....	1 30	....	....
16½	Langley Mill & Eastwood b	7 8	7 24	....	8 33	....	9 54	....	10 32	....	1 46	....	2 54	....
19	Codnor Park A	7 15	7 30	....	5 8	5 9	9 0	....	10 1	....	12 38	....	1 49	....	3 0	....
20½	Pye Bridge 681	7 23	7 34	....	8 3	9 3	....	9 26	....	10 4	....	12 42	....	1 18	1 52	....	2 12	3 5	....
23⅛	Butterley T	7 53	....	....	....	9 40	9 40	....	....	m	....	3 46	....
26¾	Ambergate 664, 702 arr	7 59	....	8 18	9 45	9 46	9 46	10 55	....	....	3 52	....
22¾	Alfreton B	7 38	7 39	8 14	5 9	....	9 49	....	10 1	....	12 48	1 24	....	3 11	....	4 56
24	Westhouses and Blackwell	7 43	....	8 18	9 13	....	10 14	....	12 52	1 28	....	3 15	....	5 0
25¾	Doe Hill	7 49	....	8 23	9 18	....	10 19	....	12 57	1 33	....	3 20	....	5 6
29	Clay Cross C 703	7 49	....	8 30	9 25	....	10 26	....	1 4	1 40	....	3 27	....	5 12
33	Chesterfield 702 arr	7 52	....	8 36	9 31	....	10 32	....	11 52	1 10	1 48	....	2 31	3 31	....	3 46	5 18	4 57

Week Days—Continued.

Miles	Station	aft	aft	aft	aft	aft	aft	aft	aft	aft	aft	aft	aft	aft	aft	aft	aft	aft	aft	mrn	mrn	mrn	mrn	mrn	aft	aft	aft	aft	aft
	642 London (St. P.) dep	2 10	....	....	2 30	....	3 25	4 25	....	3 25	....	5 0	5 0	5 32	....	6 20	6 20	....	7 50	7 50	....	....	9 30	9 45	11 50	....	1 30	3 15	....	5 0	6 15
	Nottingham ....dep	4 33	4 45	5 2	5 15	....	5 43	5 46	6	6 35	7 20	7 26	7 35	8 17	....	8 28	8	8 50	9 10	9 30	9 30	10 12	10 19	11 0	11 20	....	1 15	12 20	2 10	3 45	5 10	5 20	7 35	7 38	9 27	10 27
	Beeston	....	5 9	5 23	....	5 53	....	6 15	6 27	....	7 42	8 24	....	8 50	9 17	9 39	9 49	10 25	10 20	11 7	11 29	....	2 17	8 54	....	5 17	7 17	7 38	9 27	10 27
	Attenborough	....	5 26	....	5 57	....	6 20	....	8 54	9 21	....	10 43	11 11	11 24	....	2 21	3 53	....	9 31	10 31
	Trent 649 { arr	6 30	....	6 24	....	8 30	....	8 58	....	9 53	10 27	....	9 35	....	2 25	4	25	21	33	547	7 23	7 45	9 35	....
	{ dep	6 35	....	6 30	....	8 36	....	9 0	....	10 4	10 35	....	....	2 30	4	55	35	466	0	7 28	8	5	....
	Long Eaton	5 0	5 18	5 49	....	6 4	....	6 45	....	7 51	8 56	....	9 2	9 43	....	10 41	11 6	11 34	10 10	....	2 34	3	9	5 34	....	5 35	7 42	8	9 44	10 38
	Stapleford and Sandiacre	5 5	5 23	5 53	....	6 9	....	6 49	6 45	3 3	7 56	9 9	....	9 14	9 39	9 54	....	10 46	11 54	11 23	11 34	6 43	10 15	....	2 39	14	....	6 9	....	8 14	9 49	10 42
	Stanton Gate	....	5 27	5 56	....	....	6 45	8 0	....	9 1	....	9 37	9 54	....	10 5	....	11 5	....	....
	Trowell ....[Cossall 450	5 31	6 2	....	6 17	6 22	....	6 49	....	9 2	....	9 41	9 9	....	10 54	....	6 43	10 20	....	6 14	....
	Ilkeston Junction & 435	5 35	6 8	....	6 21	6 26	....	6 50	....	9 25	9 41	....	10 58	....	11 32	6 57	10 24	....	2 47	4	27	5 57	6 18	....	8 29	9 57	....
	Ilkeston T. ¶ { arr	5 1	6 9	....	6 24	6 5	5	56	....	8 18	....	9 30	9 44	9 10	5	....	11 1	....	11 35	....	2 50	4	25	5 50	6 18	....	8 25	10 0	....
	{ dep	4 42	6 6	9	....	8 0	....	9 10	9 11	40	....	11 40	....	....	6 12	....
	Shipley Gate ....wood	5 0	5 40	6 18	....	6 31	....	10 10	....	11 7	....	....
	Langley Mill & East-	5 4	5 44	6 22	....	6 35	....	8 15	....	9 39	....	10 21	11 48	....	7 6	10 32	....	....	6 26	....
	Codnor Park A	5 9	5 50	6 28	....	6 43	....	8 21	....	9 39	....	11 22	....	....
	Pye Bridge 681	5 14	5 54	6 31	....	6 40	....	9 42	....	10 28	11 55	....	7 14	10 40	....	....
	Butterley T 702	....	....	7 28	....	....	....	....	....	....
	Ambergate 664 arr	....	....	7 34	....	....	....	....	....	....
	Alfreton B ....[well 520	....	5 9	....	6 53	....	8 22	....	9 49	10 34	....	12 1	....	7 22	....	6 42	....
	Westhouses & Black- 524	....	5 9	....	6 57	....	8 36	....	10 38	....	....	6 46	....
	Doe Hill 5 9	....	5 9	....	8 41	....	9 53	10 3	....	7 32	....	6 51	....
	Clay Cross C 703 535	....	7 0	....	8 48	....	10 5	....	7 41	....	6 57	....
	Chesterfield 702 arr 542	....	6 25	7 16	....	8 54	....	10 53	10 35	....	12 17	7 48	....	1 21	17	....	6 25	7 5	8 20	....

A Codnor Park and Ironville.   **d** Passengers not booked from Derby to these Stations.   **B** Alfreton and South Normanton.   **B** 3 mins later Sats.
b Station for Heanor.   **C** Station for North Wingfield (⅜ mile).   **E** or **f** Exc.   † Saturdays.   **h** Except Weds. & Sats.   **m** One class only.
S or **ṣ** Sats only   **T** Butterley, for Ripley & Swanwick   **V** Via Trent   **X** Weds. & Sats.   **Y** Arr. 6 40 aft.   ‡ 10 mins later on Sats.
¶ Time on journey between Ilkeston Town and Ilkeston Junc. about 3 mins.

NOTTINGHAM AND CHESTERFIELD — June 1951

WEEKDAYS / SUNDAYS

Miles		a.m. / p.m.
	180 LONDON (St. Pancras) dep.	
0	NOTTINGHAM (Midland) dep.	
3½	Beeston	
4½	Attenboro'	
6½	Trent arr.	
	Trent dep.	
7½	Long Eaton	
9½	Stapleford & Sandiacre	
10½	Stanton Gate	
12	Trowell	
13½	Ilkeston Junction & Cossall	
16½	Langley Mill & E'tw'd for Heanor	
19½	Codnor Park & Ironville	
20½	Pye Bridge	
23	Alfreton & South Normanton	
24½	Westhouses & Blackwell	
25½	Doe Hill	
29	Clay Cross	
33	CHESTERFIELD (Midland) arr.	

Miles		a.m. / p.m.
0	CHESTERFIELD (Midland) dep.	
4	Clay Cross	
7½	Doe Hill	
9	Westhouses & Blackwell	
10	Alfreton & South Normanton	
12½	Pye Bridge	
13½	Codnor Park & Ironville	
16½	Langley Mill & E'tw'd for Heanor	
19½	Ilkeston Junction & Cossall	
21	Trowell	
22½	Stanton Gate	
23½	Stapleford & Sandiacre	
25½	Long Eaton	
26½	Trent arr.	
	Trent dep.	
28½	Attenboro'	
29½	Beeston	
33	NOTTINGHAM (Midland) arr.	
—	180 LONDON (St. Pancras) arr.	

A—Arrives Beeston at 6.11 a.m., Long Eaton at 6.26 a.m. and Ilkeston Junction at 6.50 a.m.
B—Through Carriages Newark (Castle) to Blackpool (North) (Tables 213 and 140).
C—Through Carriages Leicester (London Road) to Scarboro' (Londesboro' Road) (Tables 180 & 218).
D—Arrives Ilkeston Junction at 6.43 a.m.
E—Will not run after September 8th.
F—Arrives 3.57 a.m. on Saturday mornings and 5.9 a.m. on Sundays.
G—Through Carriages 9.40 a.m. Scarboro' (Londesboro' Road) to Leicester (London Road) (Tables 218, 216 & 180).
Starts from Scarboro' (Central) on Sept. 15th, only.
H—Arrives 10.48 a.m. on Sats.
J—Through Carriages 9.40 a.m. Blackpool (North) to Newark (Castle) (Tables 140 and 213).
L—Through Carriages Morecambe (Prom.) to Nottingham (Midland) (Tables 180 and 216).
MO—Mondays only.
S—Sunday nights only.
N—Arrives Beeston 5.52 a.m. Long Eaton 6.8 a.m. and Ilkeston Junction at 6.35 a.m.
P—Through Carriages Nottingham (Midland) to Morecambe (Prom.) until September 8th.
(Tables 216 and 180).
R—Runs to Chesterfield (Midland) only, on September 15th and 22nd.
S—Monday mornings.
V—Depart St. Pancras 11.25 a.m. on Saturdays.
Y—Arrives Stapleford and Sandiacre at 5.35 p.m.
SO—Saturdays only.
SX—Saturdays excepted.
TC—Through Carriages.
b—Stops to set down passengers.

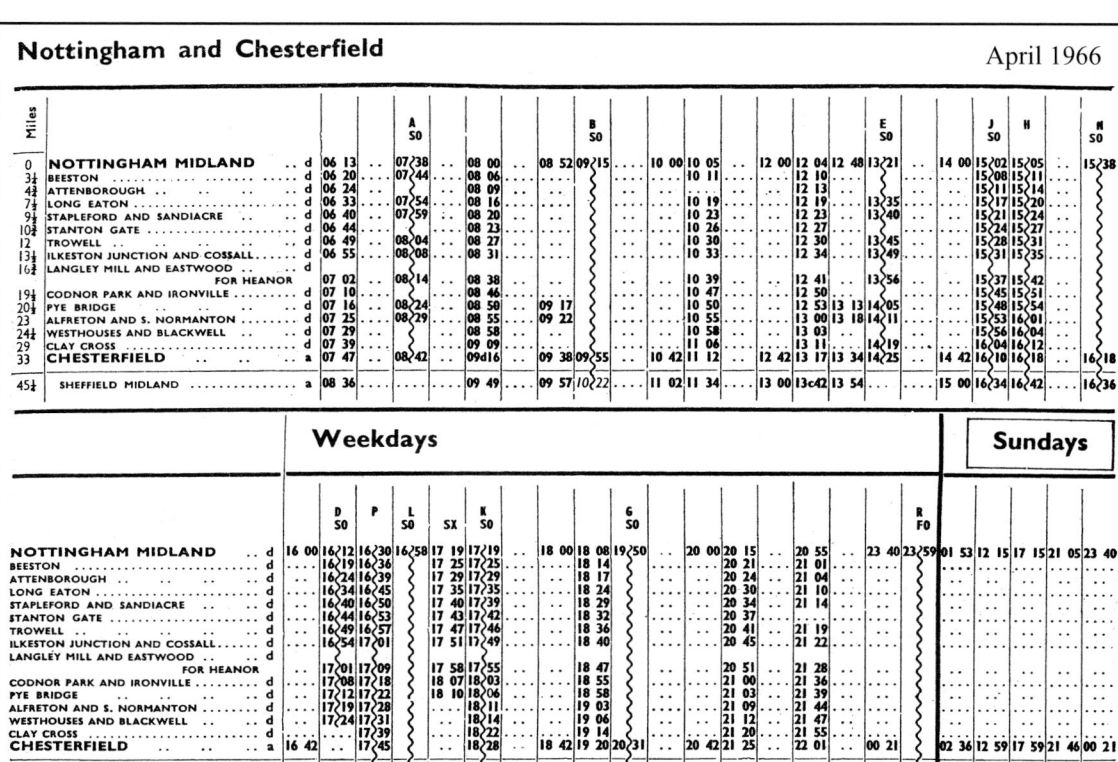

Nottingham and Chesterfield — April 1966

A 16 July to 27 August. Through carriages Nottingham Midland to Blackpool North
B 2 July to 27 August. Through carriages from Leicester London Road to Scarborough
D 18 June to 3 September. Through carriages from Skegness
E 25 June to 10 September. Through carriages from Yarmouth Vauxhall
G 18 June to 3 September. Through carriages from Portsmouth Harbour

H Not Saturdays 18 June to 3 September
J 18 June to 3 September
K 18 June to 10 September
L 25 June to 3 September. Through carriages from Poole to Bradford Exchange
N 16 July to 13 August. Through carriages from Bournemouth Central to Leeds City
P Not Saturdays 18 June to 10 September
R 1 July to 26 August

b Arr. 00 46 Sundays
c On Saturdays arr 13 46
d On Saturdays 18 June to 3 September arr 09 19

ILKESTON JUNCTION & COSSALL

II. The 1847 main line is shown as LMSR on this 1947 map, at 5ins to 1 mile. We start our journey lower right, but the platforms are north of the road bridge, as is the main building. The first station was about ¼ mile south of it, until 1870. The station near the left border can be seen on the back cover map as LNER. Known as NORTH, it served passengers from 1878 until 1964. The suffix TOWN was used on the branch terminus for most of its life, which lasted from 1847 until 1947. The Babbington branch ran to the colliery of that name from 1849 to 1903, when it was shortened, until closed in 1986. It had earlier been known as Cinderhill Colliery.

1. We look south from the end of the down through platform. The suffix 'Cossall' was added on 1st December 1890. 'Junction' preceded it on 1st July 1879. The platforms and tracks were subjected to severe subsidence in 1935, due to coal mine faults developing. The map shows the proximity of Cossall Colliery, which was active in 1868 to 1929. (R.J.Essery coll.)

2. South Junction Box was south of the road bridge; the goods lines are on the right. The junction to the north, beyond the top border of map II, was known as Bennerley Junction. Three pairs of tracks ran from the North Curve of the triangular junction for almost a mile. (M.J.Stretton coll.)

3. This view north is from an up train on 9th June 1956. Passengers for Ilkeston Town joined their train, usually one coach, behind the building. The branch carried freight until 1960, much of it being coal for the gas works. (H.C.Casserley)

4.   Class 4 2-6-4T no. 42373 is heading the 4.30pm Chesterfield to Nottingham service on 16th April 1959. Of the four running lines, the two under the far bridge span were dedicated to through goods trains. Closure came on 2nd January 1967 to passengers. There was no goods yard here, such sidings being on the Town Branch. (H.C.Casserley)

> **Ilkeston is also illustrated in our** *Loughborough to Ilkeston* **and** *Derby-Ilkeston-Nottingham* **albums. The town's street tramway can be found in the** *Ilkeston & Glossop Tramways* **volume.**

5.   The old Ilkeston station site is seen looking south from the road bridge at Bennerley. The new bridge is now roughly just past where the rear part of the train is passing on 11th March 1993. The number shown is 025 - the class is 58. (R.Geach)

ILKESTON

6.   The new station opened on 2nd April 2017. Due to improvement work at Derby, services were diverted away from there and routed via the Erewash Valley and Castle Donington route. This Cross Country service is the 09.35 Newcastle to Exeter train, with power car no. 43207 leading and it is passing the new station on 28th September 2018. The road overbridge is also new and gives access to the car park. The single goods line, once double at this point, is seen on the right. (R.Geach)

NORTH OF ILKESTON

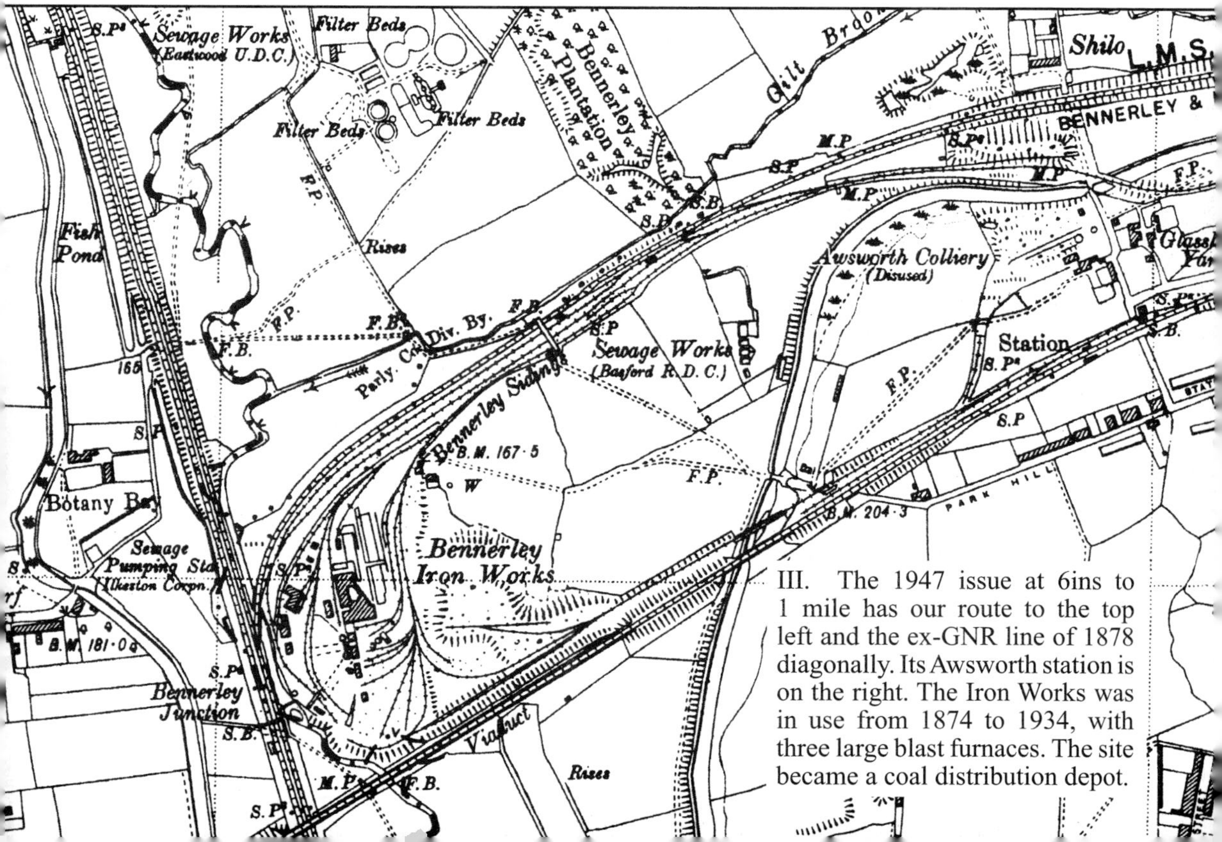

III.   The 1947 issue at 6ins to 1 mile has our route to the top left and the ex-GNR line of 1878 diagonally. Its Awsworth station is on the right. The Iron Works was in use from 1874 to 1934, with three large blast furnaces. The site became a coal distribution depot.

Bennerley Junction

7. The GNR's viaduct over the MR and the River Erewash are lower left on the map. It was 484yds in length and reached 20yds in height. Known as Bennerley Viaduct, its 16 lattice spans were built on blue brick foundations. It became listed Grade II in 1974 and carried bicycles from 1999. It is now one of only two surviving multi-span, wrought-iron, lattice viaducts in England. (R.Humm coll.)

8. A view north from the viaduct on 19th August 1983 features Bennerley Junction and a private footbridge, for staff. Class 20 Bo-Bo diesels were usually to be found working in pairs, with cabs outermost. The central boxes carried their batteries. (R.Humm coll.)

9.   The previous Bennerley Junction Box had been destroyed by one of nine German Zeppelin airships, flying low in fog to bomb Manchester on 31st January 1916. Seen on 27th August 1969, this box had 72 levers and closed on 12th October 1969. Its predecessor was built in 1900. (A.F.Bullimore)

10.   An HST headed by power car no. 43103 passes with the 16.00 Sheffield to London St Pancras on 31st July 1984. Behind the viaduct is Bennerley opencast coal disposal point, which had opened in 1983. The site had previously been occupied by Bennerley Iron Works. (P.D.Shannon)

11. No. 58028 in Trainload Coal livery is passing with the 11.50 Bilsthorpe to Staythorpe Power Station MGR coal service on 11th March 1993. On the right is Bennerley opencast loading point and rapid loader, which was used to load coal from the various opencast and reclaimed coal sites in this area. At the time of the picture, the lines look rusty, so no traffic had been in the sidings in recent times. A massive wind turbine was added to this scene in 2014. (R.Geach)

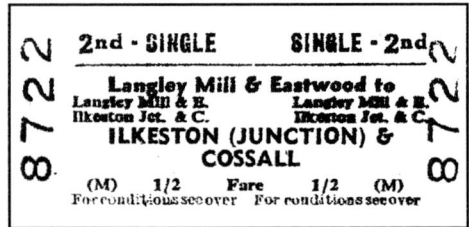

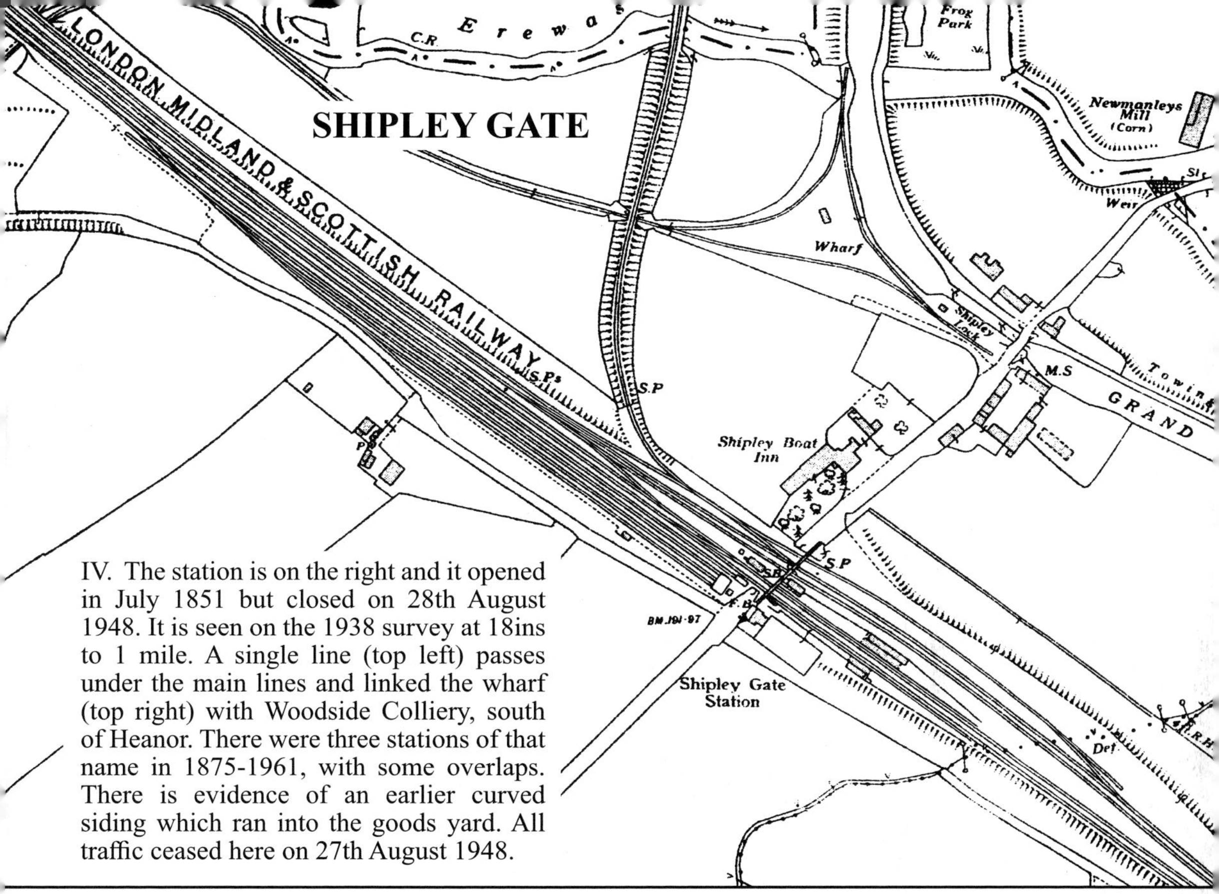

SHIPLEY GATE

IV. The station is on the right and it opened in July 1851 but closed on 28th August 1948. It is seen on the 1938 survey at 18ins to 1 mile. A single line (top left) passes under the main lines and linked the wharf (top right) with Woodside Colliery, south of Heanor. There were three stations of that name in 1875-1961, with some overlaps. There is evidence of an earlier curved siding which ran into the goods yard. All traffic ceased here on 27th August 1948.

12. The box closed on 12th October 1969 and had 32 levers. It was retained for level crossing control. Only part of one of the two gates can be seen. The WC is concealed by concrete panels. (A.F.Bullimore)

SOUTH OF LANGLEY MILL

Plain Spot

New Brinsley

Colly

Codnor Castle
(Remains of)

Lock

Codnorpark Wharf

PH

Ormonde Fields

P

Lock

Hobsick

PH

Codnor

Codnorpark Fm

Stoneyford

Locks

Brinsley Hall

Colliery (Dis)

CODNOR AND LOSCOE

Wood Linkin

PH

Brinsley

A 608

Cross Hill

A 600

Aldercar Hall

Canal

Lock

350

Cocker Ho

250

Colly

Bell Hca

A 610

Loscoe Fields

350

Aldercar

250

Lock

Eastwood Hall

New Gr

Loscoe Colly

PH

The Fall

Langley Mill

The Breach

Loscoe Grange

oe

HEANOR

Bailey Grove

Heanor Gate

P

Langley

Lock

New East

A 608 Common Side

Cemy

Marlpool

NEWTHORPE GREASLEY STA

Thorpehill Fm

Algrave Hall Fm

Old Rly

PH

Mill

Colliery

Resr

Colly

Cotmanhay Wood

200

Flatmeadow Fm

300

Prospect Fm

SHIPLEY

Cotmanhay

tehouse

Colliery

Resr

Shipley

Mapperley

Common

V. The 1950 revision at 2ins to 1 mile has the 1891 GNR line to Heanor lower left. The part shown was in use for passengers to 1929 and coal traffic until 1963. The closed station at Shipley Gate is below the words NEWTHORPE & GREASLEY STA, which was built on the GNR's Pinxton Branch and was in use in 1876-1963. Its main line is shown through Kimberley. A mineral route is marked running north from there and then west to Langley Mill, serving many collieries. Near the lowest lock is an ex-MR branch that served Digby Colliery (1854-1968) and it also carried passengers from 1882 to 1916 to Nottingham. The closed station was called Watnall; not shown is the one at Kimberley. Above that name, the route is shown as *Tk of old Rly*, that part having closed in 1916.

[continued below]

The line running west from the triangular junction south of Langley Mill also had a station at Heanor and continued off the left border to Ripley. Opened by the MR in 1890, all passenger services ceased on 4th May 1926. Goods traffic also ended west of Heanor then. East thereof most of the branch closed in 1951, and the remainder in 1971. A selection of collieries and stock are illustrated hereon. Centre on the right is Moorgreen Colliery, which was open from 1865 to 1985.

Heanor Junction

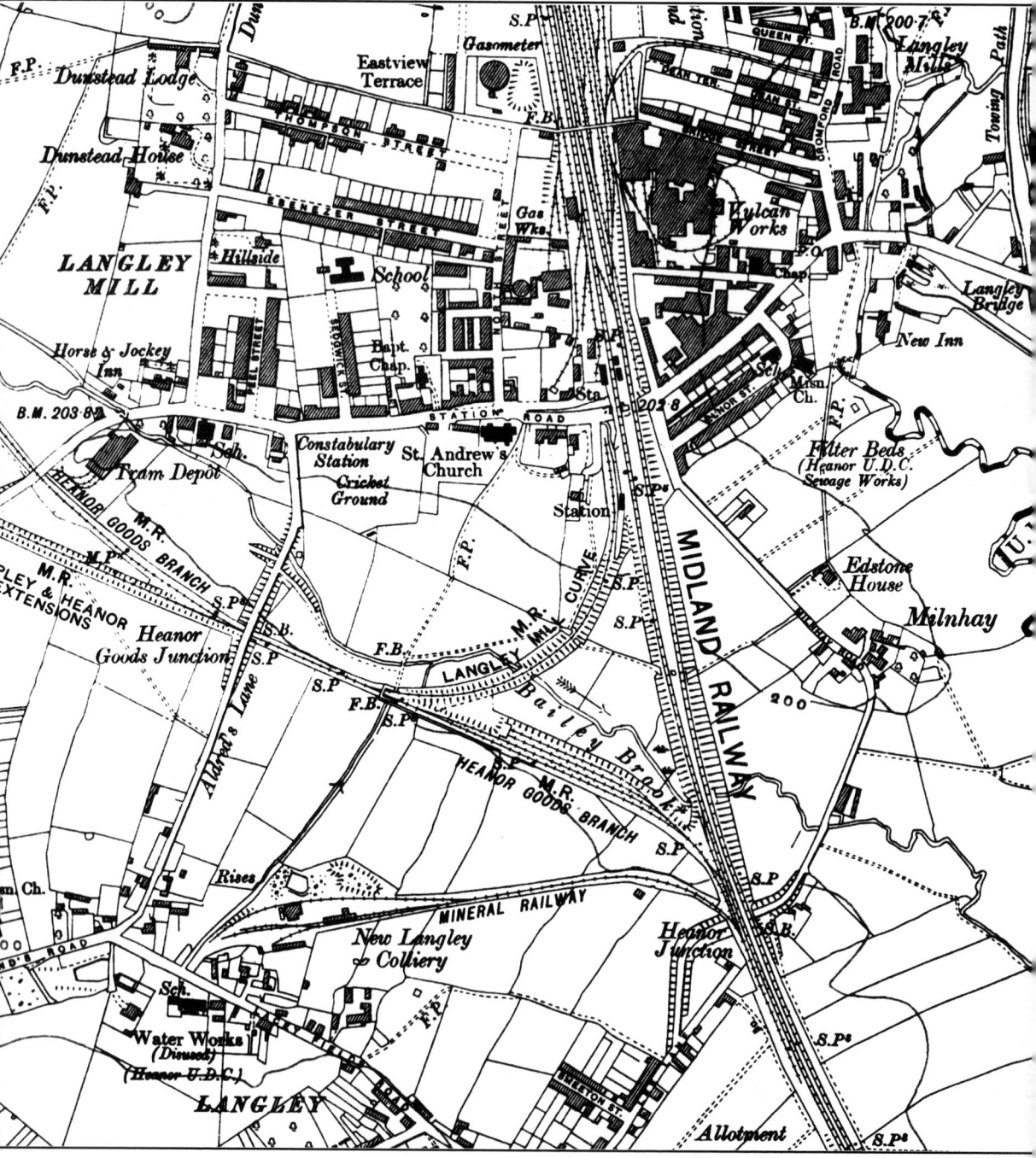

VI. The 1921 edition at 6ins to 1 mile has the junction at the lower end of the triangle. Running west from there is a privately owned single line to New Langley Colliery (1889-1960). Above this are four routes, each showing their full names.

13.   The box had 40 levers and it closed on 12th October 1969. The building was erected in 1901 to the then standard MR design. The lamp room is on the right, with an iron roof and asbestos sides. (R.Humm coll.)

14.   The New Langley Colliery Branch is seen with a train running to the Exchange Sidings on 24th April 1969. The loco is a Rolls-Royce Sentinel 0-4-0 diesel-hydraulic, built in the early 1960s. (A.F.Bullimore)

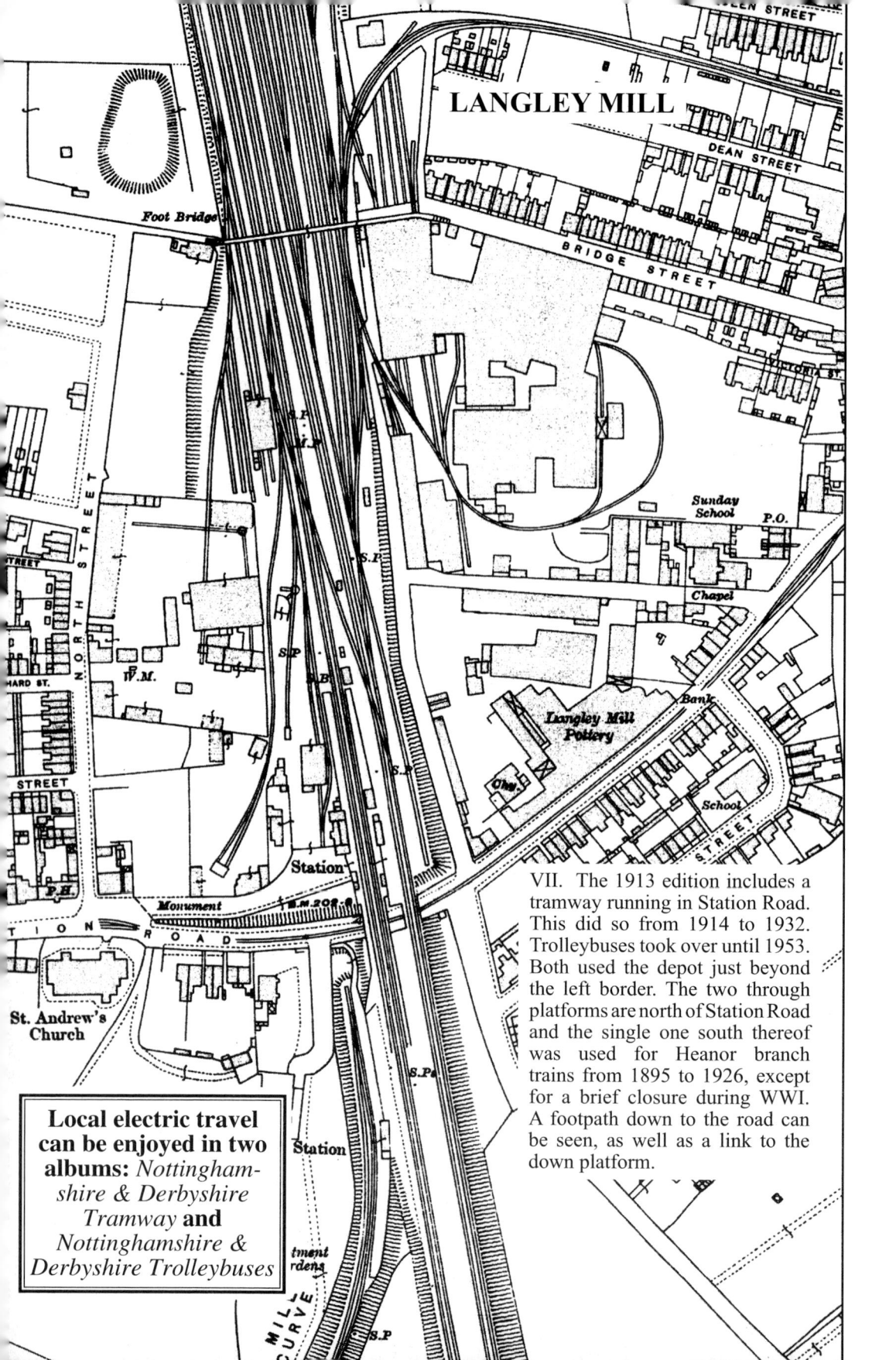

LANGLEY MILL

VII. The 1913 edition includes a tramway running in Station Road. This did so from 1914 to 1932. Trolleybuses took over until 1953. Both used the depot just beyond the left border. The two through platforms are north of Station Road and the single one south thereof was used for Heanor branch trains from 1895 to 1926, except for a brief closure during WWI. A footpath down to the road can be seen, as well as a link to the down platform.

Local electric travel can be enjoyed in two albums: *Nottinghamshire & Derbyshire Tramway* **and** *Nottinghamshire & Derbyshire Trolleybuses*

15. The station opened as 'Langley Mill for Heanor' on 6th September 1847. It is seen on 27th June 1933, with the remains of the 1895 Heanor branch trackbed in the foreground. Privately owned wagons abound. (H.C.Casserley)

16. Seen on the same day is LMS class 2P 4-4-0 no. 383. The first were built in 1882 and most were rebuilt from 1904 onwards. It is hauling the 2.30pm from Nottingham to Chesterfield. On 1st November 1876 the station was renamed 'Langley Mill and Eastwood'. On 11th September 1933 it became 'Langley Mill and Eastwood for Heanor'. (H.C.Casserley)

17. This view south is from 1951 and the end of the goods shed is on the right. Between the tracks is part of the bridge over Station Road. The two small buildings with pitched roofs cover the steps of the subway. (J.Suter coll.)

18. A northward panorama from 1952 has the goods yard on the left and to the right of the main building. Such traffic ceased on 2nd November 1964. A 30cwt crane was available. Beggerlee Branch Junction was in the right distance from 1849 to 1985. (J.Alsop coll.)

19. The prospective passenger's perspective was recorded on 15th April 1959, with the photographer's Hillman 10 featured, as coal wagons pass. The white-painted buffer stop is at the end of the goods loop, where wagons would be reversed by manpower, if no horse was available. (H.C.Casserley)

20. A two-car Derby Lightweight DMU heads past on 11th August 1962. On 2nd January 1967 the station closed and on 12th May 1986 it reopened as Langley Mill. The 1902 signal box had a 33-lever frame and it closed on 12th October 1969. (W.Taylor)

21. This is the view north from the box on 24th April 1969. Beyond the yard are Moorgreen Colliery sidings and the branch eastwards to Moorgreen Colliery, plus the sites of others. (A.F.Bullimore)

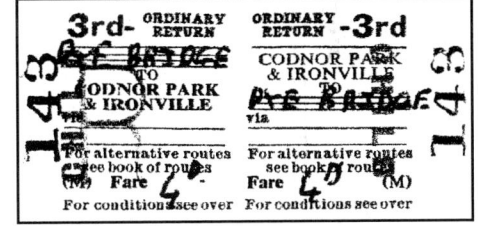

Other views of Langley Mill can be found in:
Derby-Ilkeston-Nottingham and *Ambergate to Mansfield.*

Langley Mill & Eastwood ...	Gas Light & Coke Co.'s Sid.
Barber, Walker & Co.'s Sid.	Langley Mill and Aldecar
Aldecar Siding	Co-operative Society, Ltd.,
Brinsley Colliery	Siding ....
Cordy Lane Siding	Langley Mill Co-operative
High Park Colliery	Society's Lacey Fields
Hill Top Wharf	Siding ....
Moor Green Colliery	Langley Mill Gas Co.'s Sid.
Provender Plant Siding ...	Pickersgill & Frost's Siding
Selston Colliery	Smith's Flour Mill ....
Butterley Co.—	Turner's, G. R., Wagon Wks.
Bailey Brook Colliery ...	Watnall Brick & Tile Co. ...
Heanor Lane Wharf	West, G. T., & Co.'s Siding...
Loscoe Collieries............	Langley Mill Co-operative
Loscoe Landsale Siding ...	Society's Lacey Fields Sid.
New Langley Colliery ...	Langley Mill Gas Co.'s Siding
Ormonde Colliery	

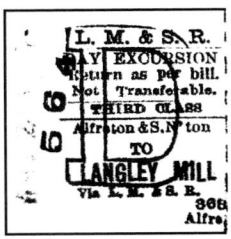

1938 sidings

22. Located slightly further south than the station that closed in 1967, the new one opened on 12th May 1986, having received financial support from Derbyshire County Council, Nottinghamshire County Council, Amber Valley District Council and five parish councils. Unit no. 170106 calls with the 13.57 Norwich to Liverpool Lime Street on 1st September 2005. (P.D.Shannon)

23. East Midlands Trains' unit nos 156405 and 158858 pass platform 2 with the 10.52 Liverpool-Norwich service on 7th November 2013.. The staggered platforms are separated by the bridge across Station Road, the A608. The annual passenger figures grew from 95,158 in 2012-13 to 121,442 in 2016-17. (A.C.Hartless)

NORTH OF LANGLEY MILL

Stoneyford Junction

24. The village of this name is top left on map V, but the old branch is shown with dashes. This 1902 box had 28 levers and is seen in 1965. Closure came on 16th February 1969. (A.F.Bullimore)

Moorgreen Colliery

25. The colliery was owned by Barber Walker & Co Ltd before nationalisation in 1947 and was probably the oldest coal mining company in the UK, with origins going back to 1680. As part of a major modernisation scheme begun in 1946, it was decided to introduce locomotive haulage in a major new seam being developed, using the track gauge of 3ft 6in. Hudswell Clarke built two new 1900 H.P. locos for the mine, the first ever of this size, and the first one was *Pioneer*. It is now preserved in Leeds Museum. (A.Neale coll.)

26. No. 24 was built by R&W Hawthorn in 1883 and survived until 1963. Its photo was taken in about 1952. The village is in the centre of the right page of map V. The colliery closed in 1985 and was involved with some opencast work for a while. (A.Neale coll.)

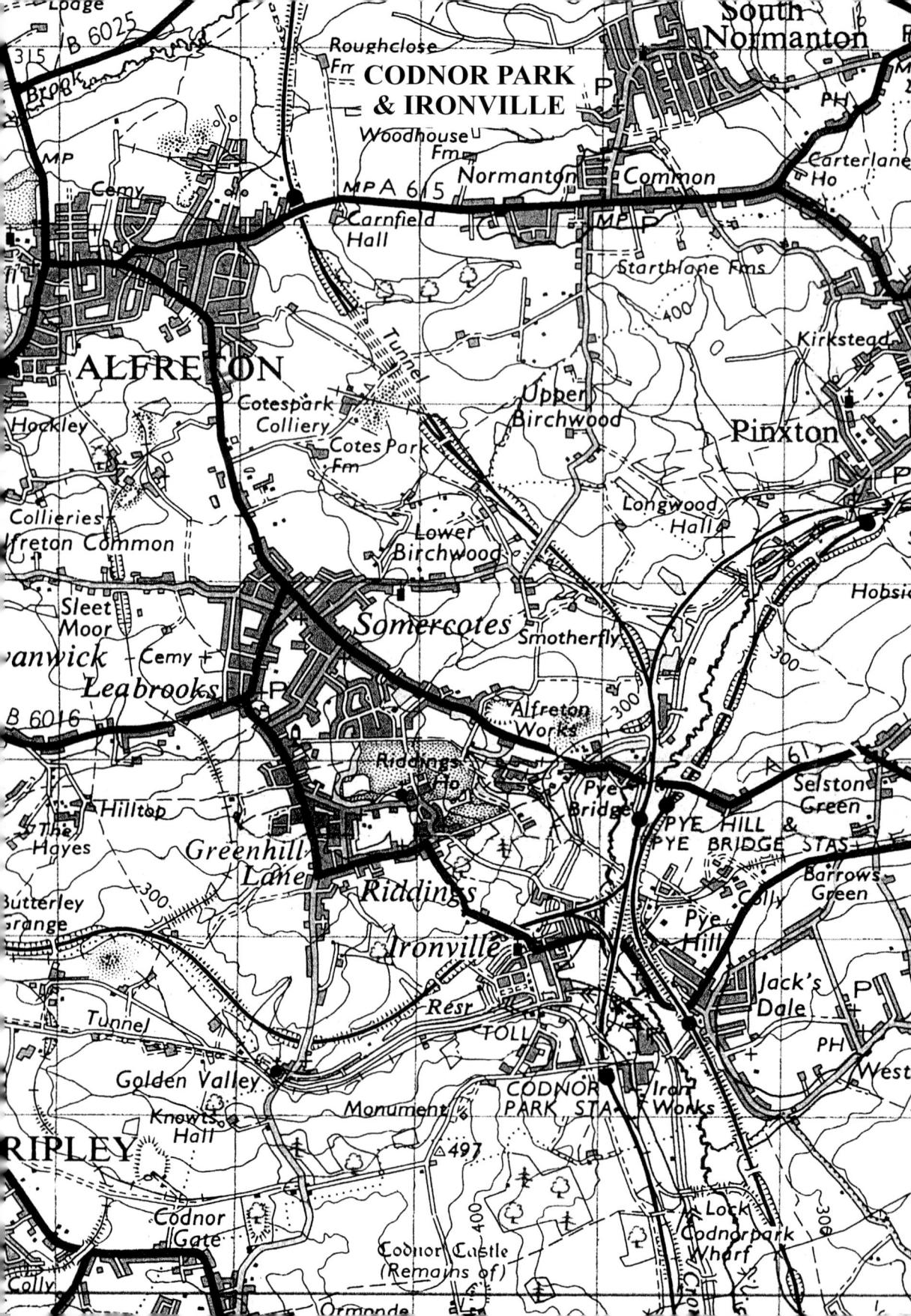

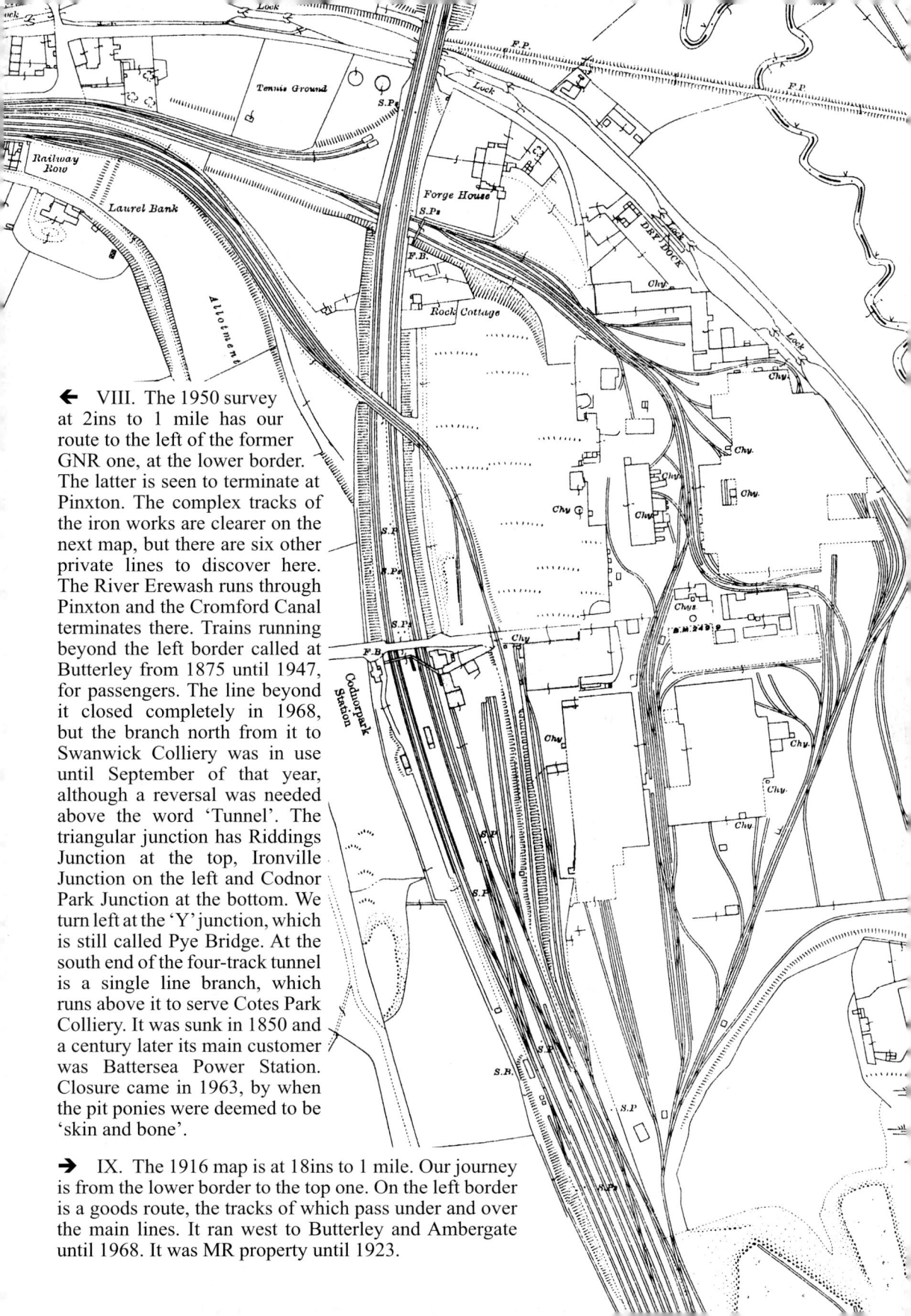

← VIII. The 1950 survey at 2ins to 1 mile has our route to the left of the former GNR one, at the lower border. The latter is seen to terminate at Pinxton. The complex tracks of the iron works are clearer on the next map, but there are six other private lines to discover here. The River Erewash runs through Pinxton and the Cromford Canal terminates there. Trains running beyond the left border called at Butterley from 1875 until 1947, for passengers. The line beyond it closed completely in 1968, but the branch north from it to Swanwick Colliery was in use until September of that year, although a reversal was needed above the word 'Tunnel'. The triangular junction has Riddings Junction at the top, Ironville Junction on the left and Codnor Park Junction at the bottom. We turn left at the 'Y' junction, which is still called Pye Bridge. At the south end of the four-track tunnel is a single line branch, which runs above it to serve Cotes Park Colliery. It was sunk in 1850 and a century later its main customer was Battersea Power Station. Closure came in 1963, by when the pit ponies were deemed to be 'skin and bone'.

→ IX. The 1916 map is at 18ins to 1 mile. Our journey is from the lower border to the top one. On the left border is a goods route, the tracks of which pass under and over the main lines. It ran west to Butterley and Ambergate until 1968. It was MR property until 1923.

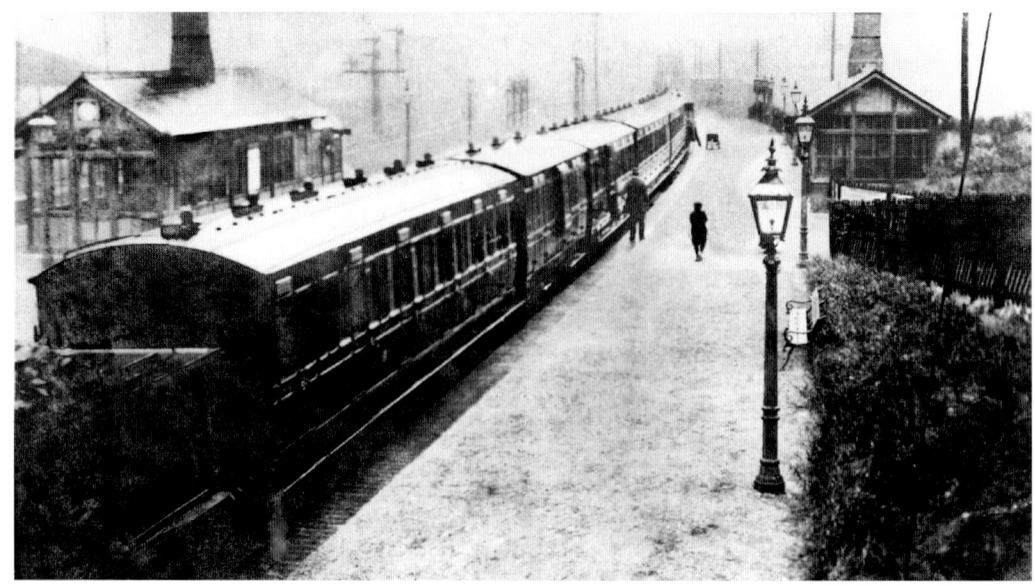

27. This early postcard producer felt that coaches were of more interest than engines, as were the backs of members of staff. At least we can enjoy one massive hearth and one shiny seat. (LOSA)

28. The suffix IRONVILLE was added on 17th November 1898 to reflect the expanding industry. This card was posted in February 1907 and includes part of one of the Iron Works. The other hearth is also given unusually good presentation. (J.Alsop coll.)

Codnor Park and Ironville ...
Butterley Co.—
Brand's Siding ....
Britain Colliery ....
Butterley Iron Works ...
Codnor Park Iron and Wagon Works (Mexborough Siding) ....
Codnor Park (for Ironville and Jacksdale) ....
Butterley Co.'s Codnor Park Iron Works & Wagon Works (Brinsley Sidings)

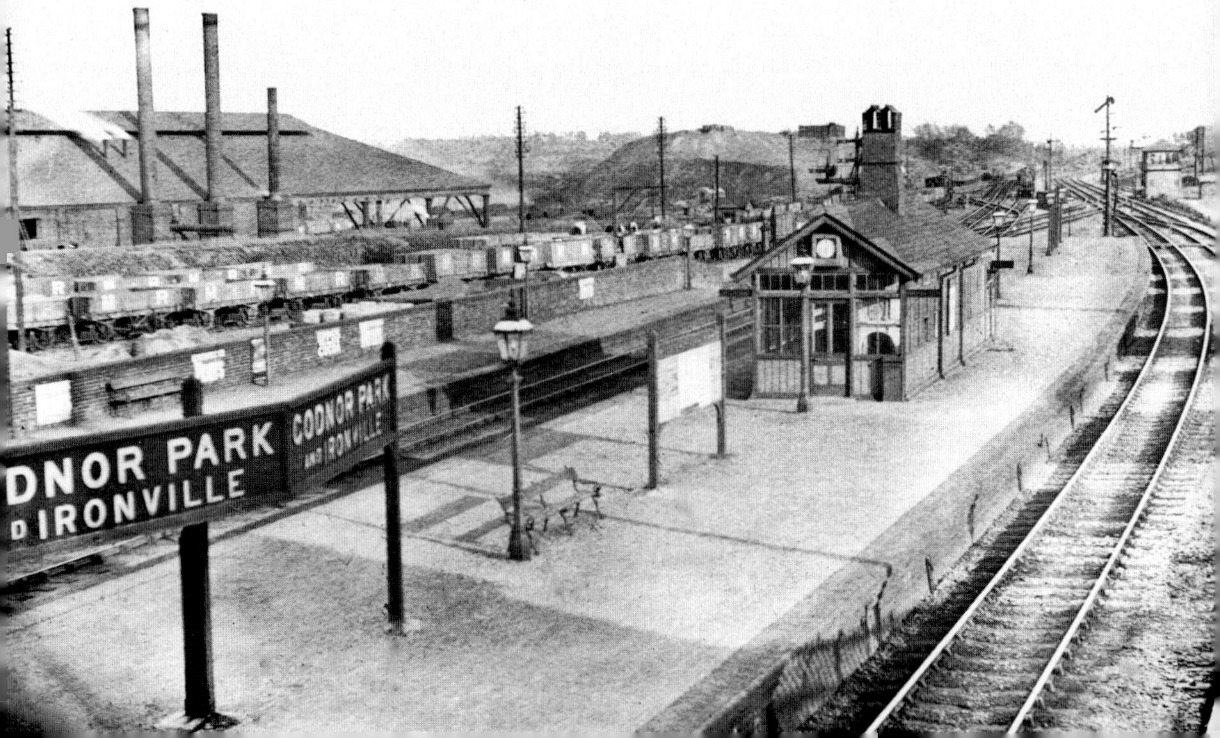

Oakes & Co.—
Collieries ....
Riddings Brick Yard......
Riddings Colliery (L.N.E.)
Riddings Sanitary Pipe Works ....
Stanton Iron Co.'s Alfreton Iron Wks. (Riddings Sids.)
Codnor Park Iron & Wagon Works (Mexborough Siding)
Codnor Park Ir n Works and Wagon Wks. (Brinsley Sids.)

(1938 sidings)

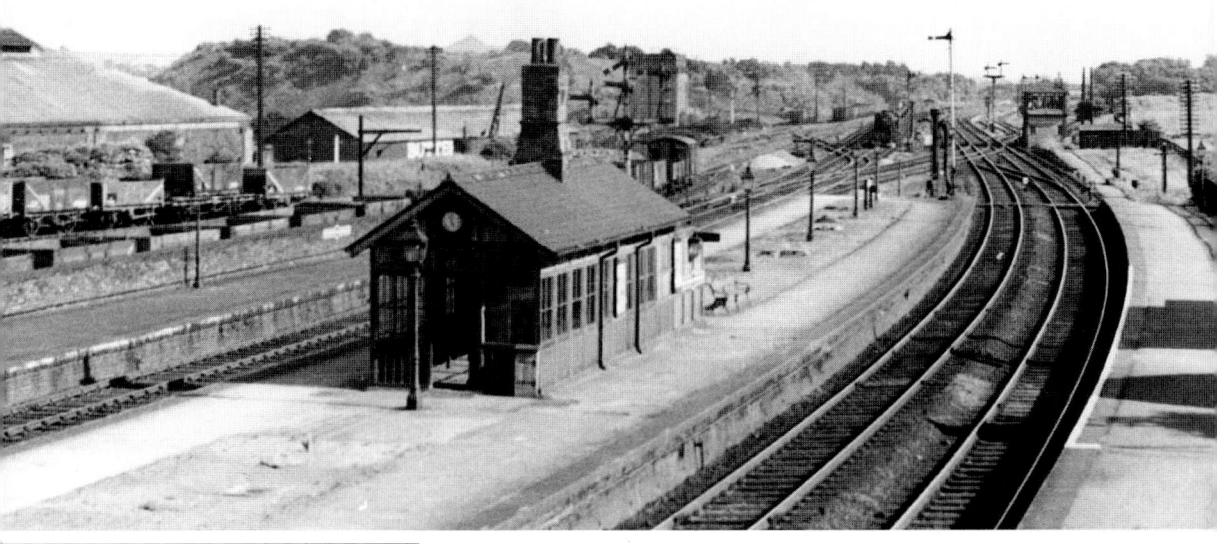

29. A 1951 panorama records busy sidings. Inward traffic included not only much iron ore, but large quantities of lime and coke needed for the production of steel. Included is the signal box, which was in use from 1902 until 1969. (R.Humm coll.)

30. Unlike many stations on the main line, four platforms were provided here, instead of two. Behind the railway observers is no. 42349, a class 4 2-6-4T, ex-LMS. The date is probably Summer 1959, when this loco was briefly shedded at Hasland. (J.Suter coll.)

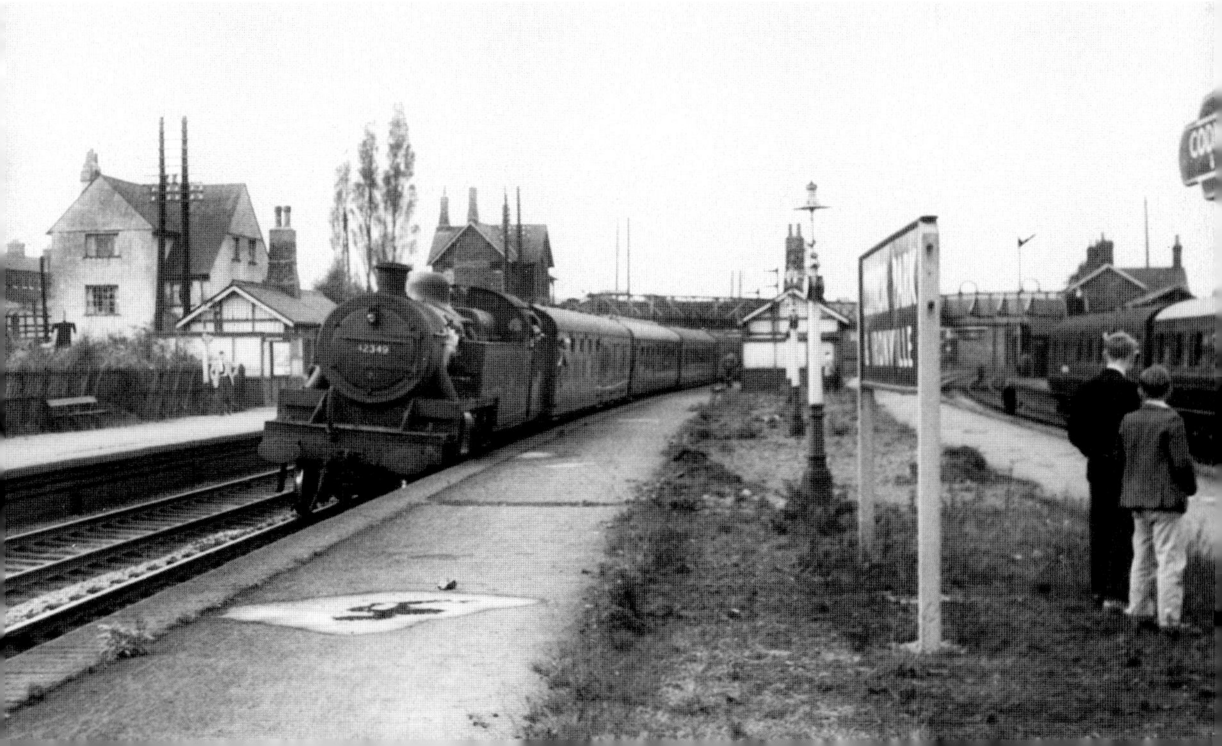

31. Southbound on 19th September 1959 is the RCTS 'Notts & Derbyshire' special, officially known as the East Midlands Branch Rail Tour. It is headed by class 2 2-6-2T no. 41320 and the station's water tank was about to be obscured by it. (R.J.Buckley/Initial Photographics)

32. Both spans of the footbridge and the full length of the road bridge were recorded on 23rd December 1966. Closure to local goods traffic came on 2nd November 1964 and to passengers on 2nd January 1967. (R.Humm coll.)

NORTH OF CODNOR PARK

Codnor Park Junction

33.   Seen on 15th March 1965 is the 55-lever box, which came into use in 1954 and closed on 12th October 1969. Mostly flat bottom rails are in place here by then. (A.F.Bullimore)

Codnor Park Sidings

34.   No. 56006 waits with MGR wagons loaded with coal on 22nd April 1992. From December 2001, there was one such train daily to Ratcliffe Power Station. It also had regular supplies from Bentinck Colliery. (R.J.Stewart-Smith)

SOUTH OF PYE BRIDGE

Riddings Junction

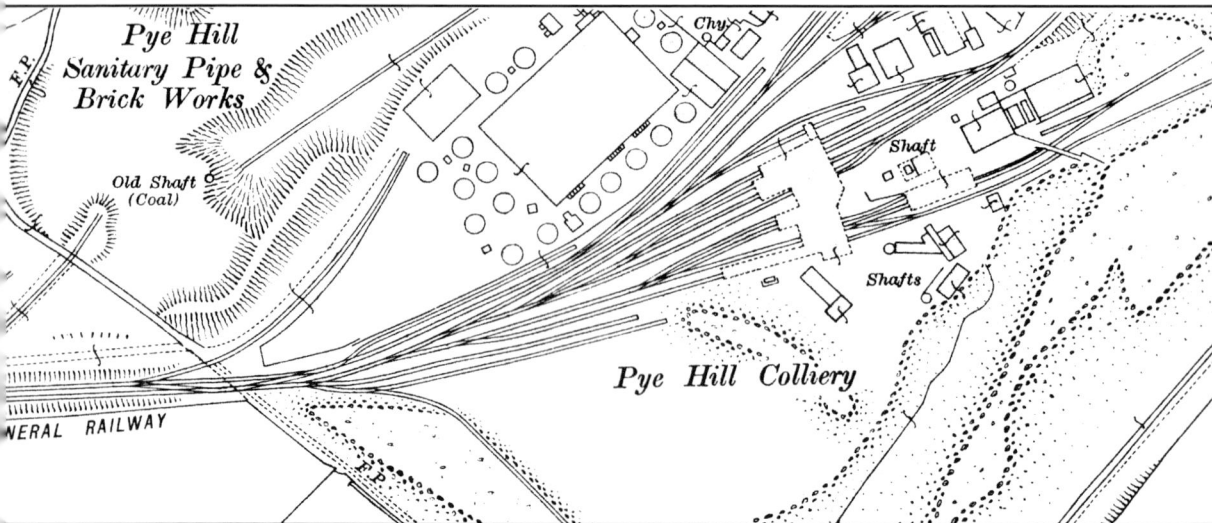

35. The location of the triangular junction can be found on map VIII and Riddings is west of it. Waiting for its signal sometime in 1960 is class 4 4-6-0 no. 75064. The name is lower left on map XI opposite and passing under all the lines there is the single track serving most of the firms in the 1938 sidings table, lower right. (D.Pearce coll.)

X. These sidings were served by the track passing under the main lines, below those seen lower left on map XI. The scale is down to 18ins to 1 mile.

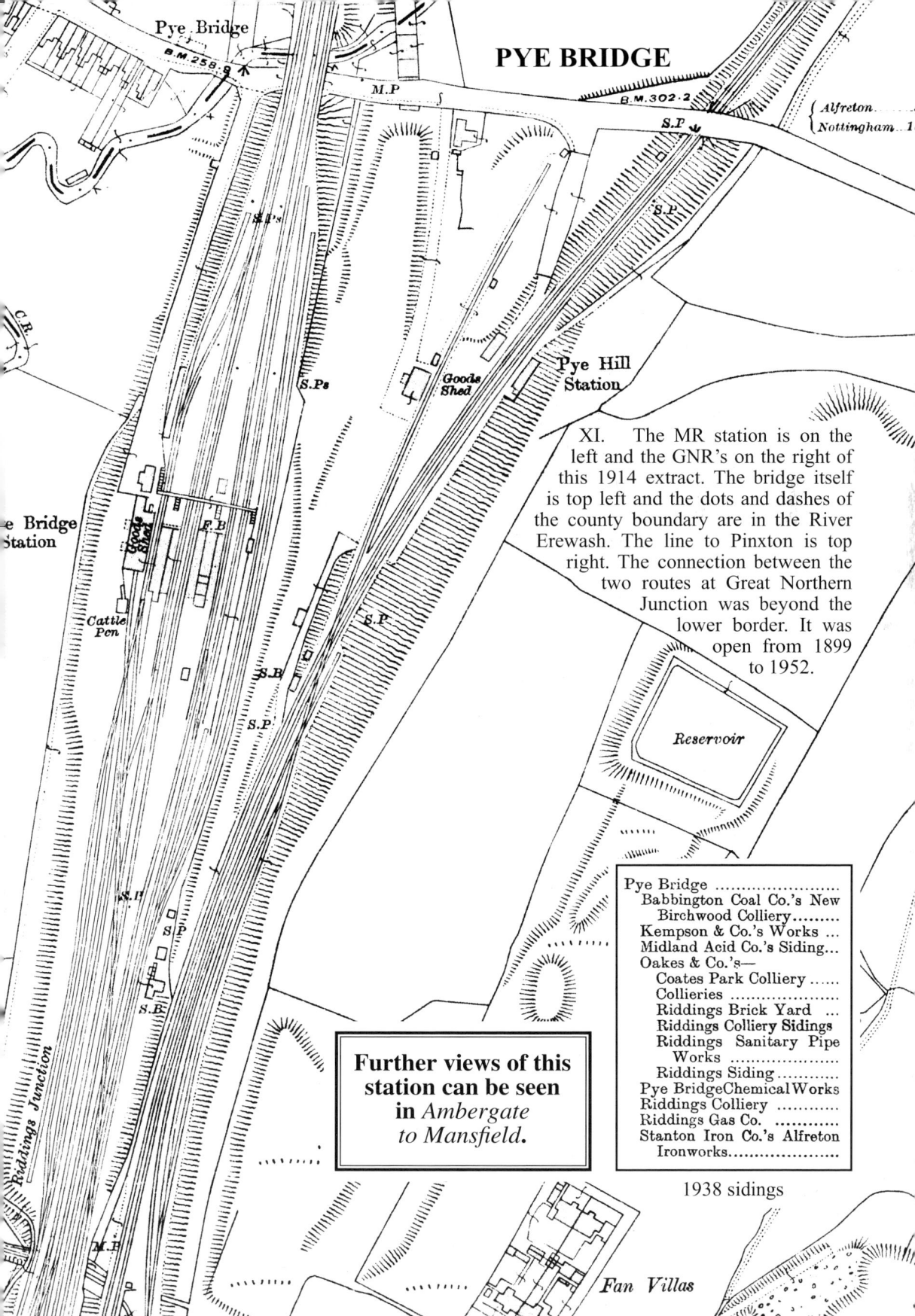

Pye Bridge

BM 258.8

PYE BRIDGE

M.P

BM 302.2

{ Alfreton
Nottingham 1

S.P

S.P

S.P

C.R.

S.P^s

Goods
Shed

Pye Hill
Station

XI.   The MR station is on the
left and the GNR's on the right of
this 1914 extract. The bridge itself
is top left and the dots and dashes of
the county boundary are in the River
Erewash. The line to Pinxton is top
right. The connection between the
two routes at Great Northern
Junction was beyond the
lower border. It was
open from 1899
to 1952.

e Bridge
Station

Goods
Shed

F.B.

S.P

Cattle
Pen

Reservoir

S.B.

S.P

S.P

S.P

S.P

Riddings Junction

S.B.

M.P.

| Pye Bridge |
| Babbington Coal Co.'s New Birchwood Colliery |
| Kempson & Co.'s Works |
| Midland Acid Co.'s Siding |
| Oakes & Co.'s— |
| Coates Park Colliery |
| Collieries |
| Riddings Brick Yard |
| Riddings Colliery Sidings |
| Riddings Sanitary Pipe Works |
| Riddings Siding |
| Pye Bridge Chemical Works |
| Riddings Colliery |
| Riddings Gas Co. |
| Stanton Iron Co.'s Alfreton Ironworks |

**Further views of this
station can be seen
in** *Ambergate
to Mansfield.*

1938 sidings

Fan Villas

36. A northward panorama from about 1947 has the owners' names still on most of the coal wagons. Cotes Park Colliery and its waste tip are in the left background. Access to it was by a line laid over the top of Alfreton Tunnel. (D.Pearce coll.)

37. Running in on 3rd July 1954 with a Chesterfield to Nottingham stopping train is no. 40557, a class 2P 4-4-0. The train will have been down a 1 in 230 incline through Alfreton Tunnel. (R.Humm coll.)

38. The station was built close to the east bank of the River Erewash and thus on soft ground. This explains the need for lightweight platforms on stilts. A class 3F 0-6-0 is shunting a mixed train on 2nd September 1955. (R.M.Casserley)

39. Another view north on the same day and this includes the goods shed. The yard had a 5-ton capacity crane and closed on 2nd November 1964. There is more evidence of flowerbed reconstruction. (R.M.Casserley)

40. We look south on 27th February 1960 as class 8F 2-8-0 no. 48552 creeps through with empties. The crossing was for staff and parcel traffic. The station was open to passengers from 1st December 1851 until 2nd January 1967. (R.Humm coll.)

41.   The date is 10th September 1962 and no. 45589 is working an up goods train. It is a Jubilee class 4-6-0 and was named *Gwalior*. The shed on the left was for staff bicycles and motorbikes. The signal box in the distance was used in 1892-1969. (W.Taylor)

NORTH OF PYE BRIDGE

Coates Park South

42.   The signal box of that name was recorded in 1966. The box had opened in 1902 with 32 levers and was closed on 12th October 1969. The denseman's hut is centre. It was used by staff in dense fog at night to make safety observations. (A.F.Bullimore)

43.   Reference to map VIII (after picture 26) will help locate these views. This one is above 'Lower Birchwood', which is near Somercotes, centre. A short branch curves left, before reaching the cutting. Barely visible is the line to Cotespark Colliery as it passes over the bridge, above the hollow on the right; only its fences are visible. (Note, 'Cotespark' is one word on the 1950 map.) It then climbs along the right side of the cutting, in shrubbery, and then passes over the tunnels. The rod runs to the detonator placer. In the distance is Coates Park North box. (A.F.Bullimore)

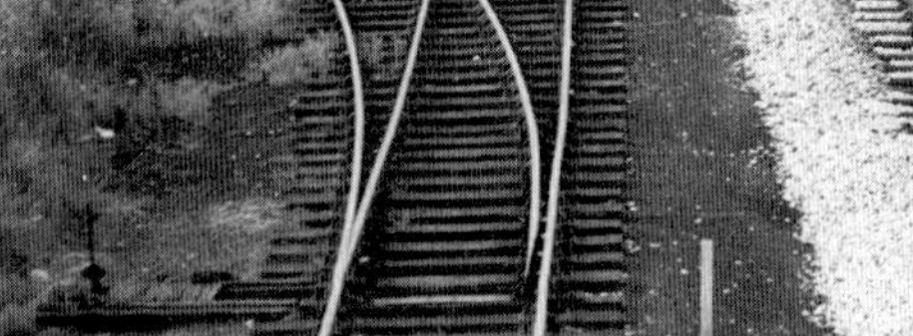

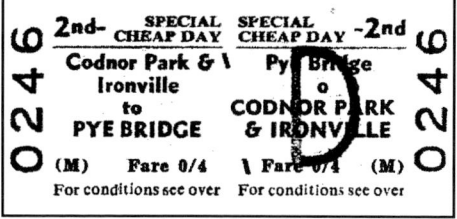

Coates Park North

44. This view south from above the tunnels has the footpath passing over four tracks and then taking a Z-bend over a bridge across the single line, just described. Running north on 1st June 1963 is class 8F 2-8-0 no. 48331, with a mixed freight. (R.J.Essery coll.)

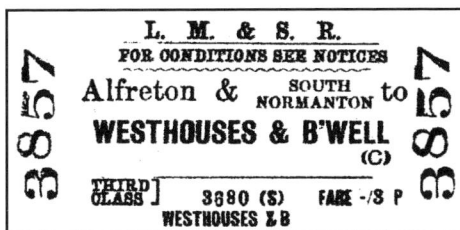

L. M. & S. R.
FOR CONDITIONS SEE NOTICES
Alfreton & SOUTH NORMANTON to
WESTHOUSES & B'WELL
(C)
THIRD CLASS 3680 (S) FARE -/3 P
WESTHOUSES & B
3857

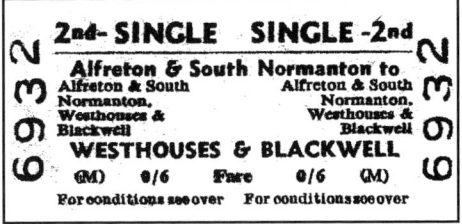

2nd- SINGLE   SINGLE -2nd
Alfreton & South Normanton to
Alfreton & South Normanton, Westhouses & Blackwell   Alfreton & South Normanton, Westhouses & Blackwell
WESTHOUSES & BLACKWELL
(M)   0/6   Fare   0/6   (M)
For conditions see over   For conditions see over
6932

Alfreton Tunnel

45. An 0-6-0 approaches the south portal of the eastern tunnel. The fencing of the single line passes over it, as do the uninsulated telephone wires. The early MR signal arm has a sighting board behind it. (R.Humm coll.)

46. Both southern portals can be seen better in this photo from 19th October 1963. The up goods train is hauled by class 8F 2-8-0 no. 48391. There were over 600 of these successful engines in use. The first tunnel is on the right and both were built to an 840yd length, with three ventilation shafts each. The second one was opened in 1901 and the first closed circa 1970. (W.Taylor)

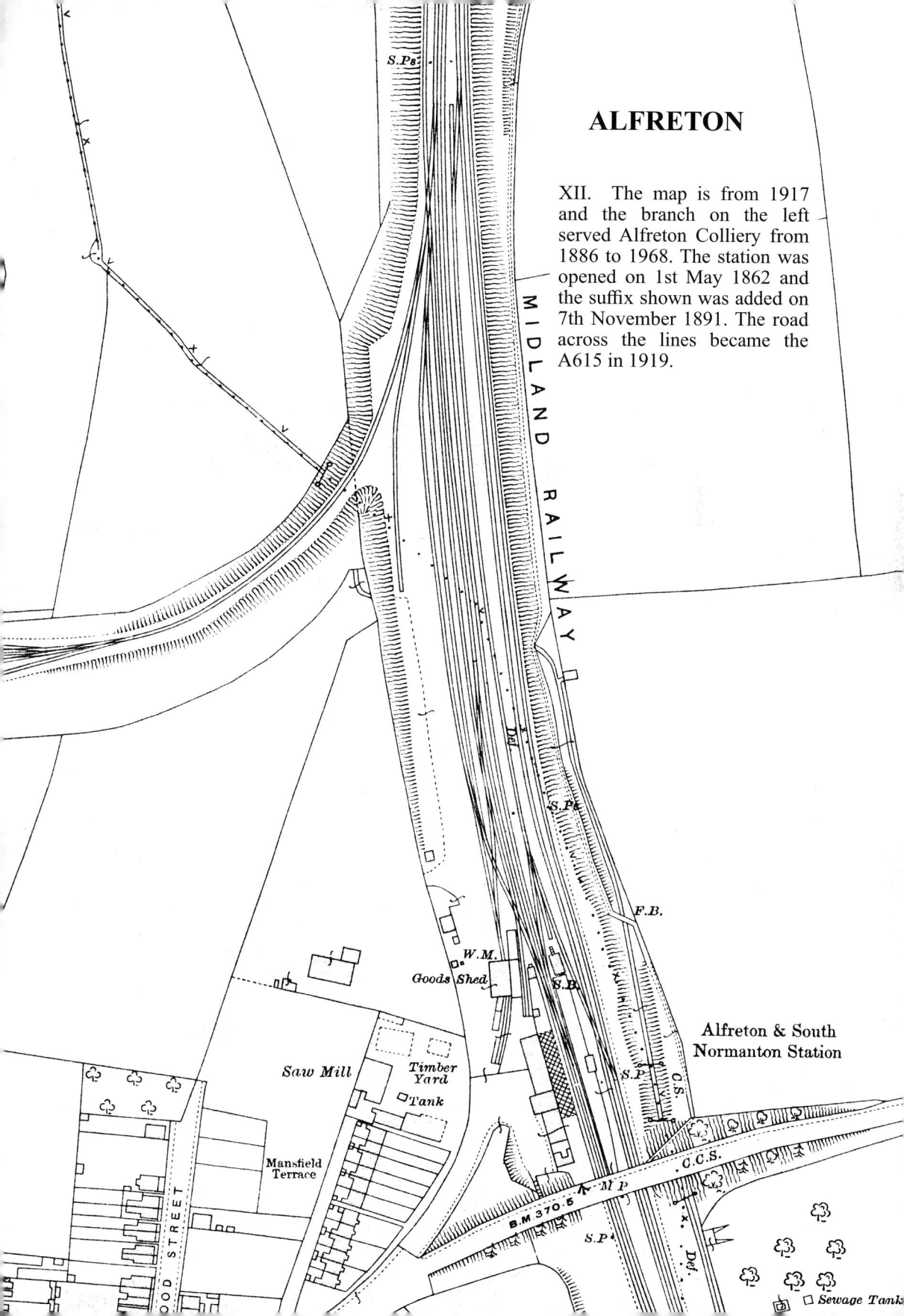

ALFRETON

XII. The map is from 1917 and the branch on the left served Alfreton Colliery from 1886 to 1968. The station was opened on 1st May 1862 and the suffix shown was added on 7th November 1891. The road across the lines became the A615 in 1919.

MIDLAND RAILWAY

Saw Mill

Timber Yard

Tank

Mansfield Terrace

Goods Shed

W.M.

S.B.

F.B.

Alfreton & South Normanton Station

Sewage Tank

B.M. 370.5

47. The splendid styling was recorded on a postcard in about 1900. The ornate iron brackets were probably cast locally. The population grew from 17,505 in 1901 to 23,020 in 1961. (J.Alsop coll.)

48. Another early card reveals two more splendid facia boards, together with local commercial transport of the period. This also provided free fertiliser for domestic gardens, when needed. (P.Laming coll.)

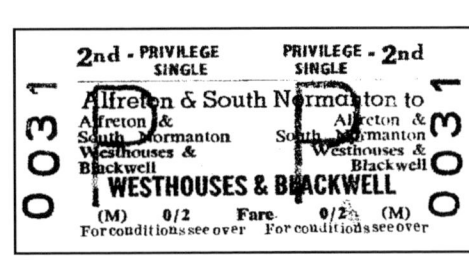

2nd - PRIVILEGE SINGLE   PRIVILEGE - 2nd SINGLE
0031
Alfreton & South Normanton to
Alfreton & South Normanton Westhouses & Blackwell   Alfreton & South Normanton Westhouses & Blackwell
WESTHOUSES & BLACKWELL
(M) 0/2   Fare.   0/2   (M)
For conditions see over   For conditions see over
0031

49. Passenger train parcel traffic was very varied and close examination of large baskets of the type seen here could reveal fresh fruit and/or vegetables, plus live poulets about to embark on a training course in egg laying. The annotation is curious as some letters appear back-to-front. (J.Alsop coll.)

50. A view south on 27th February 1960 features class 4F 0-6-0 no. 44070 and more local parcels. Such items often had to be pulled over the staff crossing and up the steep platform ramp, on a large trolley. (R.J.Essery coll.)

↑ 51. A panorama northwards from the road bridge on 23rd June 1961 includes no. 43850, a class 4F 0-6-0, which was a type introduced by the MR in 1911. The town became well-known for the production of chocolate, by Thorntons, for decades. (R.J.Essery coll.)

→ 52. The frame had 36 levers and closure came on 12th October 1969. It had started work in 1901. This wider view from 1968 shows the changes since the platforms had closed on 2nd January 1967. The goods yard closed on 2nd October 1967 and engineers were using it. (A.F.Bullimore)

↗ 53. Alfreton & Mansfield Parkway is seen on 16th July 1983. It had opened on 7th May 1973. No. 47483 calls with the 10.16 Barrow-Nottingham at 14.26. This short-lived service was a replacement for the daily Glasgow-Nottingham through train. Note the trackbed of the former goods lines to the right. This was the second Parkway station in the UK; the first was near Bristol. There were through peak-hour trains to and from London here. (A.C.Hartless)

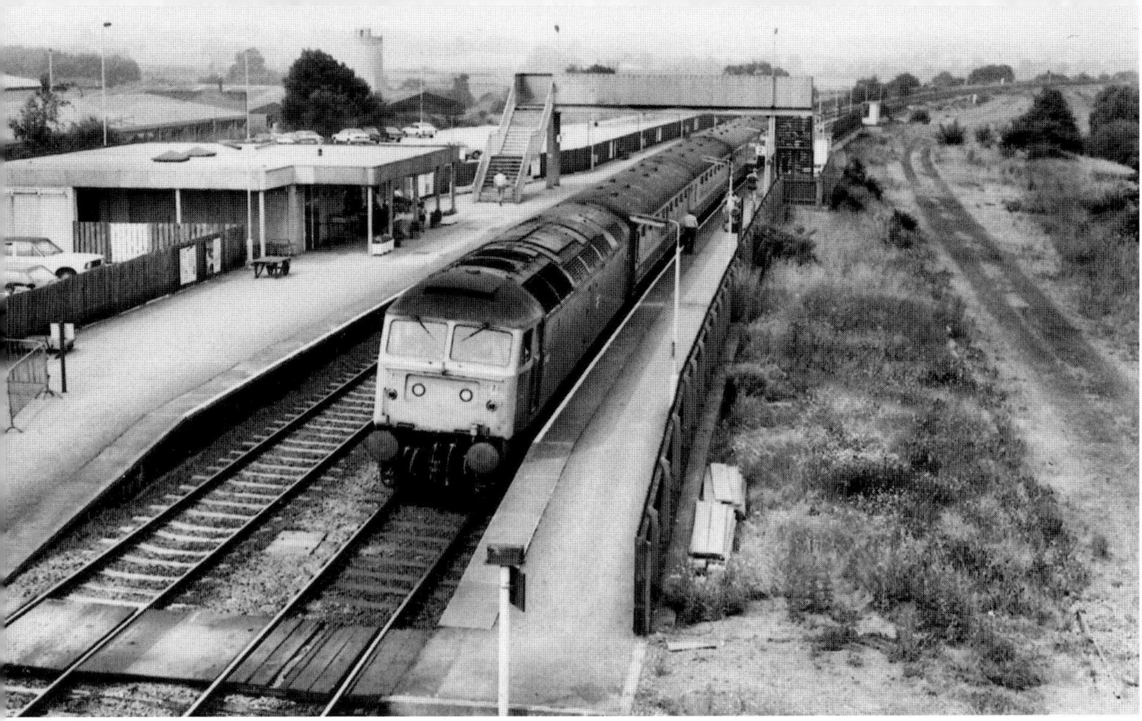

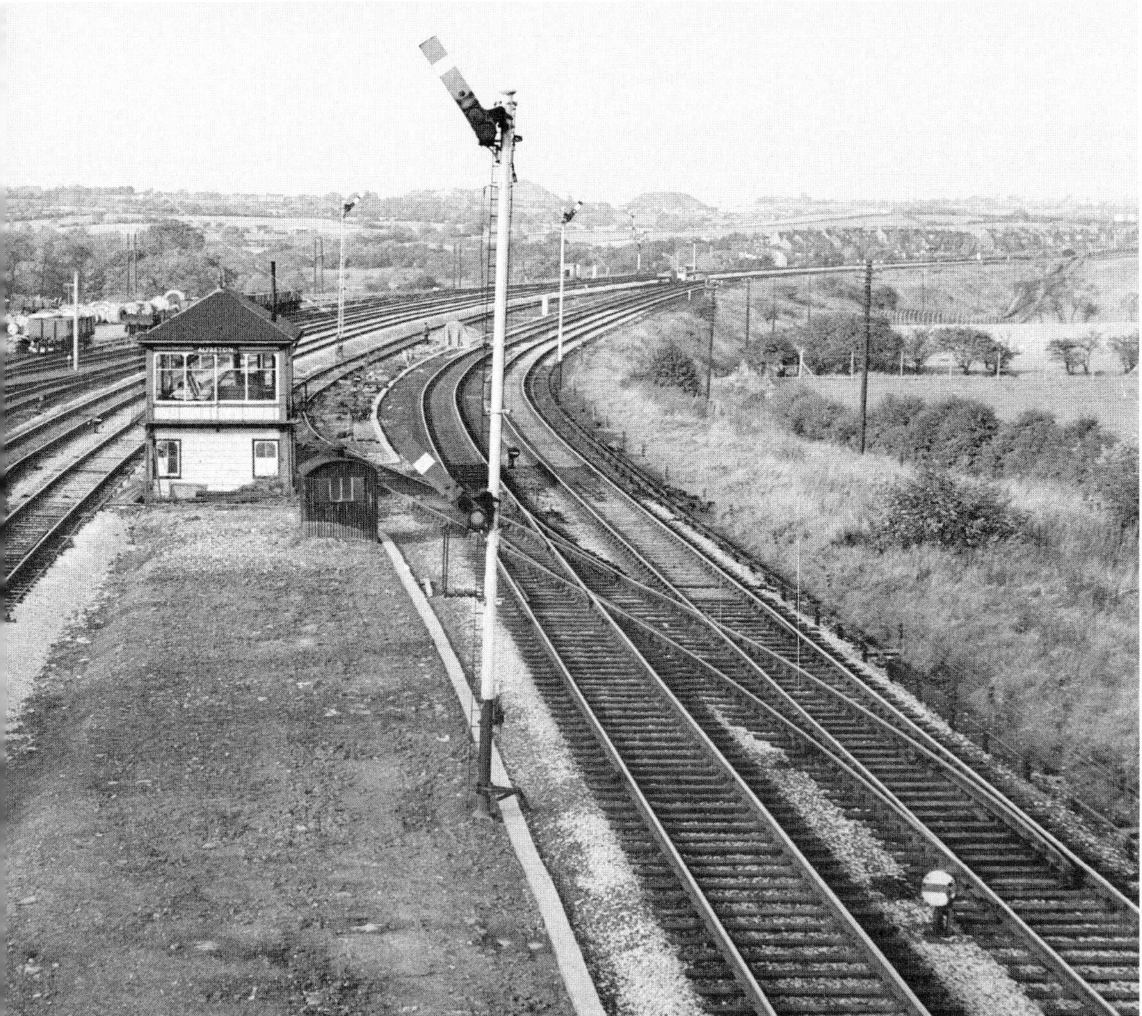

54. It is evident on 23rd May 1990 that the old platforms had come into use again. No. 56026 is southbound with loaded MGR wagons. Mansfield regained its own station on 20th November 1995 and its name was removed from here. Details are in our *Mansfield to Doncaster* album. (T.Heavyside)

55. This panorama is from 22nd August 2013 and the white structure, beyond the tree, is the footbridge. The station was provided with a ticket office and toilets. The car park could accommodate 200 cars. (R.Geach)

56. It is 28th September 2018 and East Midlands Trains no. 158858 is leading a class 156 unit and forms the 10.52 Liverpool Lime Street to Norwich. At Nottingham the class 156 will be detached and the 158 will continue onwards to Norwich on its own. This view is from the footbridge. Platform 2 had a small waiting shelter at the foot of the steps. (R.Geach)

0310 2nd - CHARTER CONTROL E.M.T.A. Saturday, 20th September, 1975 Alfreton & Mansfield Parkway to BLACKPOOL AND BACK 0310 (M)   (M) For conditions see over   For conditions see over

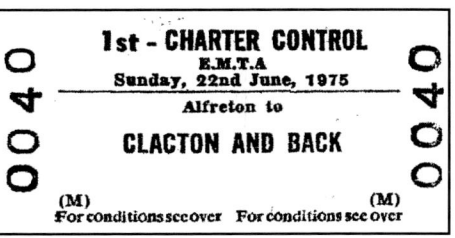

0040 1st - CHARTER CONTROL E.M.T.A Sunday, 22nd June, 1975 Alfreton to CLACTON AND BACK 0040 (M)   (M) For conditions see over   For conditions see over

57. We have seen the start of the half-mile long branch to Alfreton Colliery on the last map. This is an inter-war picture. During and after World War II, those young men refusing to shoot others were ordered to dig coal for the nation's benefit instead. This was in addition to Mr Bevin's Act of Parliament. Your author (VM) was one of them, but escaped into medical school instead. (Bevin Boys Assoc.)

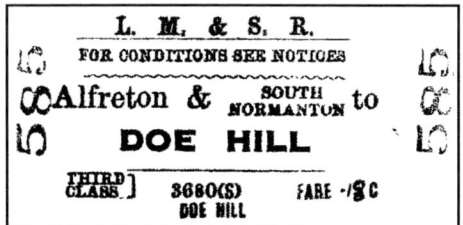

L. M. & S. R.
FOR CONDITIONS SEE NOTICES
Alfreton & SOUTH NORMANTON to
DOE HILL
THIRD CLASS]   3680(S)   FARE -/8 C
DOE HILL

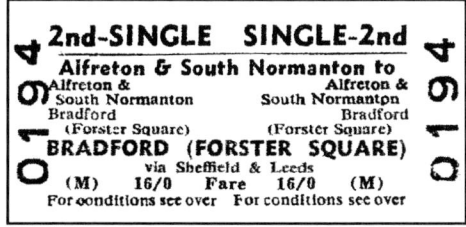

2nd-SINGLE   SINGLE-2nd
Alfreton & South Normanton to
Alfreton &   Alfreton &
South Normanton   South Normanton
Bradford   Bradford
(Forster Square)   (Forster Square)
BRADFORD (FORSTER SQUARE)
via Sheffield & Leeds
(M)   16/0   Fare   16/0   (M)
For conditions see over   For conditions see over

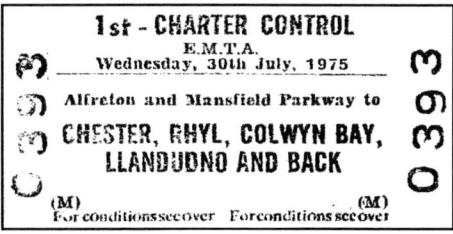

1st - CHARTER CONTROL
E.M.T.A.
Wednesday, 30th July, 1975
Alfreton and Mansfield Parkway to
CHESTER, RHYL, COLWYN BAY,
LLANDUDNO AND BACK
(M)   (M)
For conditions see over   For conditions see over

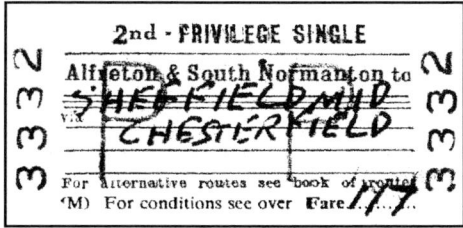

2nd - PRIVILEGE SINGLE
Alfreton & South Normanton to
VIA SHEFFIELD MID
CHESTERFIELD
For alternative routes see book of routes
'(M) For conditions see over Fare 1/7

Church Hill

epinorno ane

Opencast Mining

Seanor Fm

Broomridding Wood

Parkhouse Green

Hardstoft Common

Parkhouse Fm

Waterloo

PH

Hardstoft

PH

Danesmoor

Colliery

Colliery

Biggin Fm

Bushypark Fm

enhagen Fm

P

Inn

Reservoir

Pilsley

The Cedars

Padley Wood

Pilsley Green

Lane End

PH

Overmoor

Padleywood Fm

Pewithall Fm

Sitwell Grange

Hagg Ho

Westwood Brook

P

PH

Nethermoor

Colliery

B 6014

DOE HILL STA

B 6025

Tibshelf

Colliery (Dis)

orton

Doehill Ho

St Thomas's Row

Tk of Old Railway

P

P

Stonebroom

Newton

PH

Mount Pleasant

Scanderlands

Primrose Hill

Sewage Wks

PH

Blackwell

Westhouse Fm

P

WESTHOUSES & BLACKWELL STA

P

Westhouses

Blackwell Hall Hilcote

Blackwell Colliery

Normanton Brook

Shirland

XIII. The 1950 edition is shown at 2ins to 1 mile. Our route is from the lower border to the top left corner, from where Clay Cross is two miles. Two areas of opencast working of coal are shown. The GCR route is on the right. It was opened in 1892 and closed in 1968.

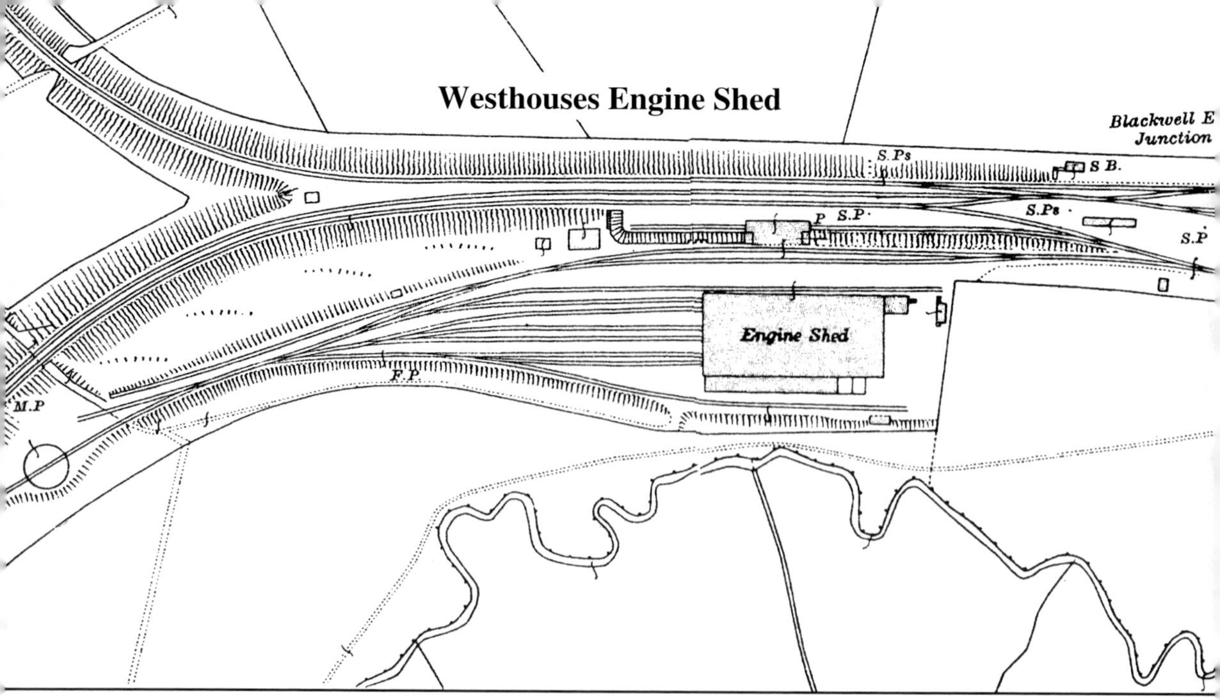

Westhouses Engine Shed

Blackwell E
Junction

S.Ps · · S B.

P S.P. · S.Ps ·

S.P

Engine Shed

F.P.

M.P

XIV. This is dated 1917 and is an enlargement of the centre part of the next map, which is opposite picture 64. The lines to Blackwell Colliery and New Hucknall Colliery are on the right. The upper line was in use from 1877 to 1984. The others were briefer. The turntable had a limited life, as the later larger engines were turned on the triangle seen on the next map.

↗ 58. A fine panorama from 8th July 1951 includes the water and coal supplies on the left. The shed code was 18B in 1948-63 and 16G in 1963-66. There were 61 locos allocated here in 1950 and 19 in 1959. (R.Humm coll.)

→ 59. This view is from 14th July 1966; the shed officially closed on 3rd October 1966. The white columns would have been of value during the black-out restrictions of WWII. Water supply problems limited the growth of this depot in steam days. (D.Pearce coll.)

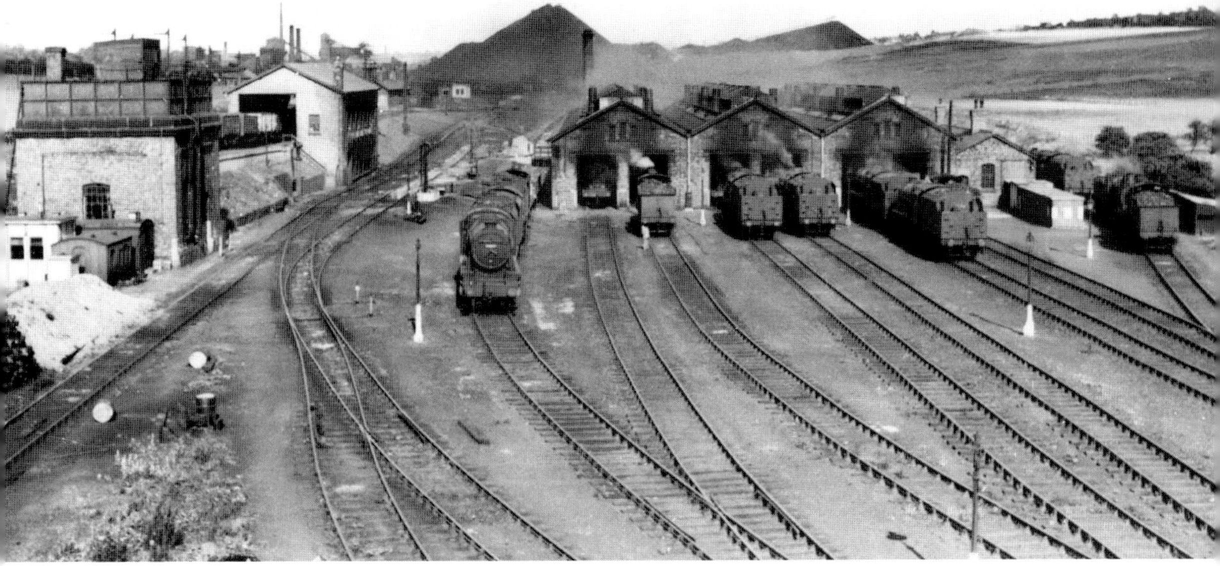

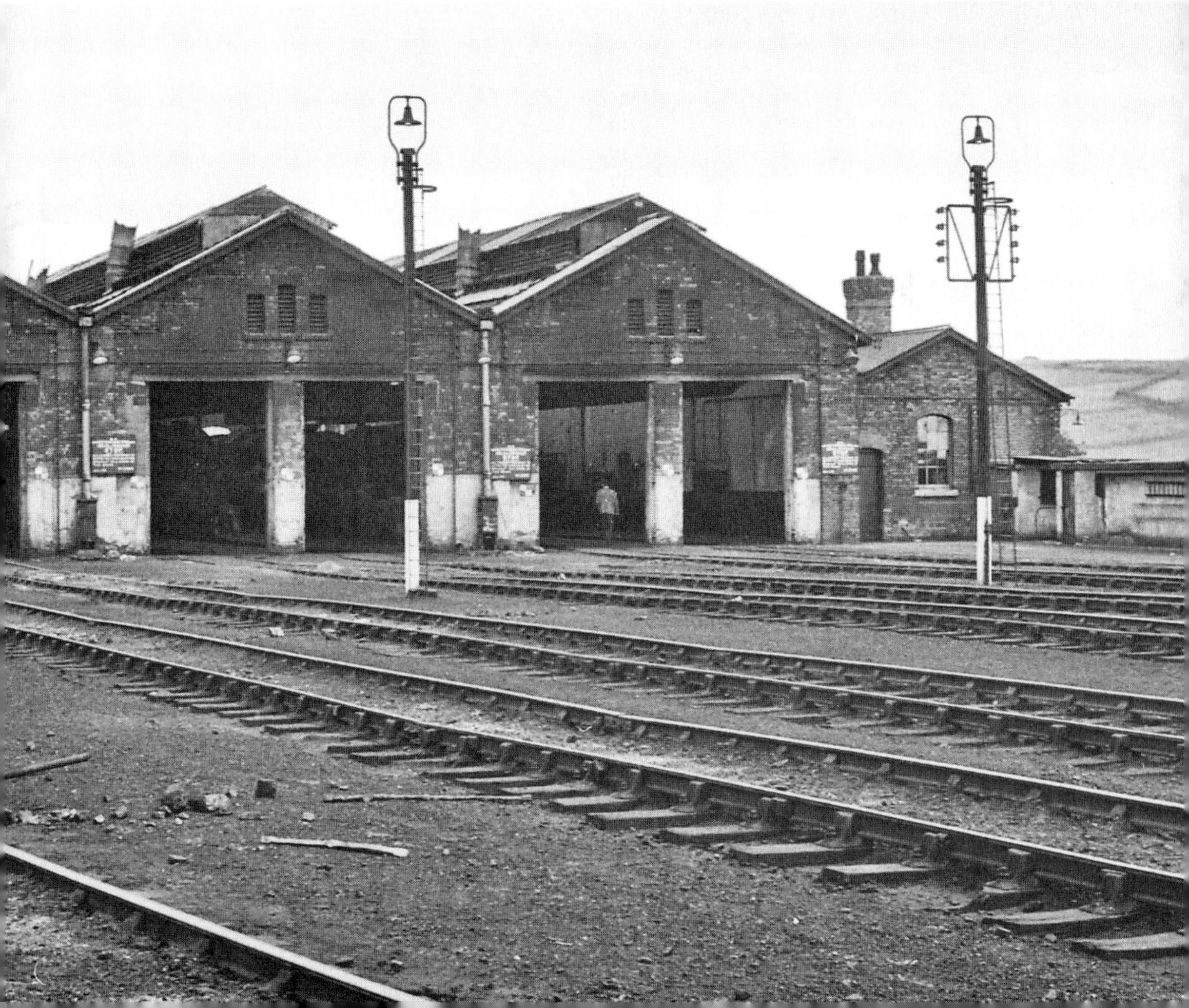

60. Class 11s were here briefly. Classes 20, 25, 47 and 56 were present until 1986. This is the selection on offer on 27th March 1967, with their train reporting numbers on display. The old coaling stage is still standing on the left. (Colour-Rail.com)

61. Three pictures from 25th September 1983 follow and this one includes two diesels, plus a van berthed in the open. The large water tank towers remain as a link with the steam era. The code WU was used from May 1973 to January 1975 for the Motive Power Depot. (R.J.Stewart-Smith)

Blackwell East Junction

62. On the right is the remaining single line to the MPD, dropping steeply. Reversal was needed. The short signal arms are for calling-on purposes, using line of sight. (R.J.Stewart-Smith)

63. A view in the other direction completes the story. The water tank appears again. A later diagram, from 1990, showed a siding south of here serving the Alfreton Explosives & Chemical Company. (R.J.Stewart-Smith)

New Hucknall Colliery

64. No. 1 *Portland* was Yorkshire Engine Co no. 325 and was built in 1878. It is seen in March 1956. The flat top to the water tank was to give the fireman stability when filling it. (A.Neale coll.)

65. This panorama is from 10th June 1978. The shaft was sunk in 1874-76 and closure came in 1982. This view is from the final years, after flood lighting had been invented. It aided shunting greatly. (A.J.Booth)

WESTHOUSES & BLACKWELL

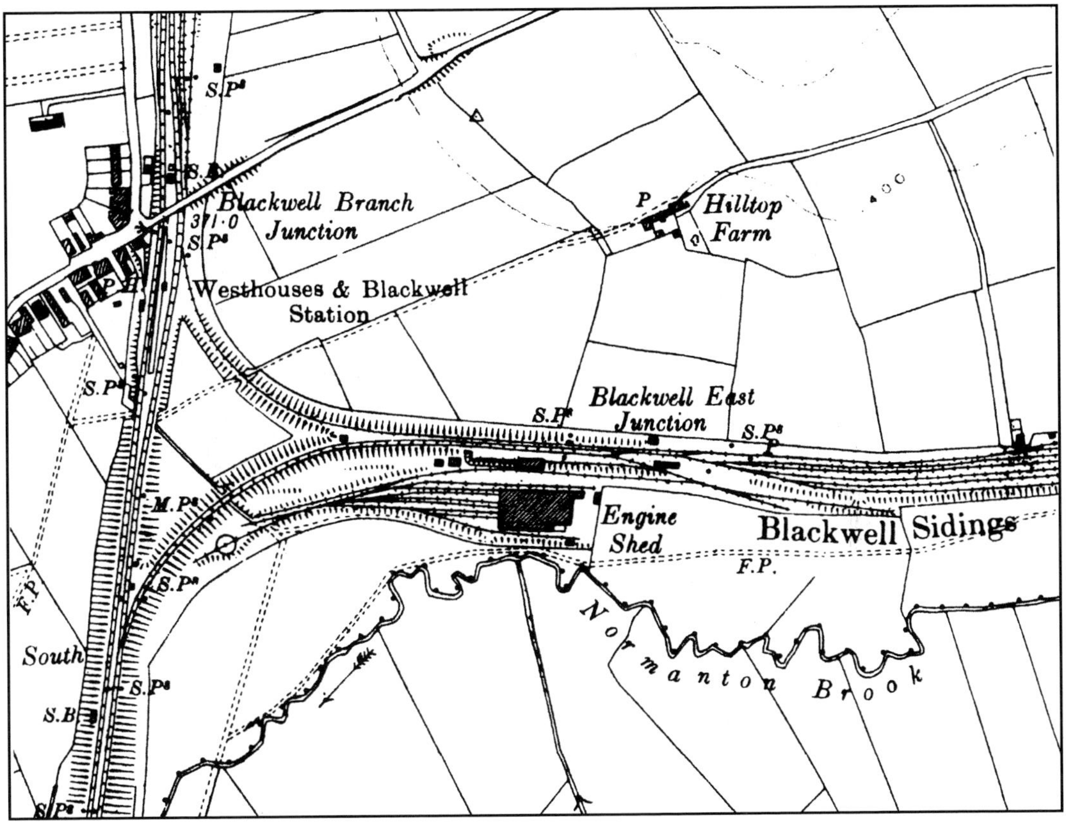

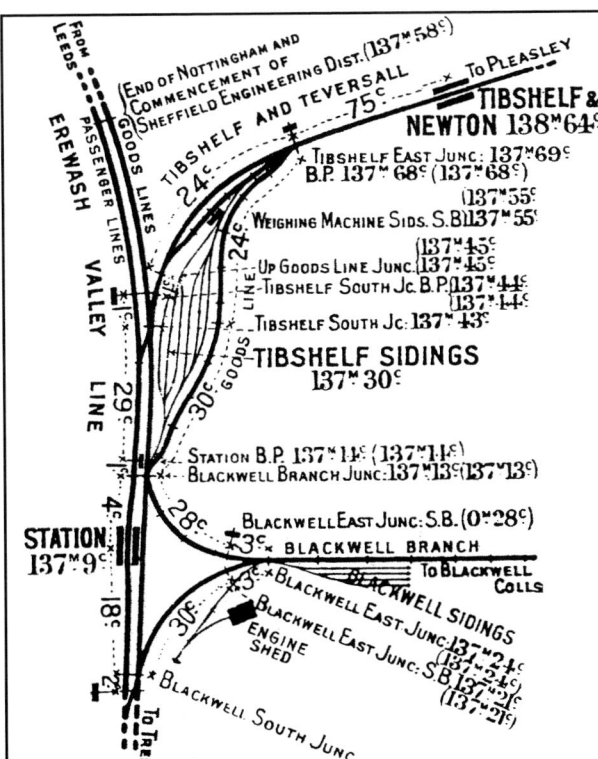

XV. Above is the 1921 issue at 6ins to 1 mile and the station is south of the main road, but the platforms are not clear. The signal box is north of the road bridge. The 1913 MR diagram, left, shows miles and chains in profusion.

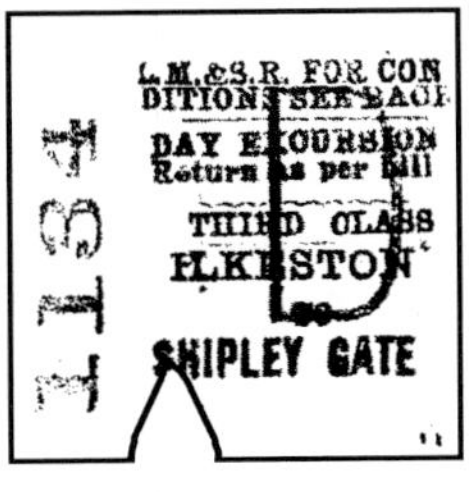

66.   The last map shows the platform south from the road bridge. The road was unnumbered, but the B6025 curved close to the west side of the station from 1919. The station opened on 1st May 1862. It was called West House and closed on 1st August 1865, having been open on Saturdays only. (P.Laming coll.)

67.   The station reopened as 'Westhouses & Blackwell' on 17th October 1881. Another postcard features the original brick arches. The MR was the main employer in the district and even built the local school, but mains electricity was not available before about 1950. (J.Alsop coll.)

68.   Passing through, devoid of a train, on 11th June 1955 are two class 4F 0-6-0s, nos 44605 and 44229. Gas lights prevailed here, to the end. Steel spans were provided over the goods lines when laid and those on the left came later. (Milepost 92½)

69.   At the far end of the sidings, a branch line ran to Tibshelf, Sutton, Silverhill, Butcherwood and Pleasley collieries. Part is shown on map XIII. It carried passengers until 1930 and became a footpath more recently. No. 92114, a class 9F 2-10-0, is about to pass under the road. The local goods yard is behind the left signal. (R.J.Essery coll.)

HOUSES & BLACKWELL

70.   This was the Railway Correspondence & Travel Society's 'Notts and Derbyshire Rail Tour' on 19th September 1959. It was propelled by class 2 2-6-2T no. 41320. The signals on the right are for down goods trains. The local goods service ceased on 2nd November 1964. (R.Humm coll.)

71.   Blackwell South Junction is in the distance as a DMU departs with a Sheffield to Nottingham service on 13th August 1965, while a coal train leaves the Blackwell Branch. Passenger service ended here on 2nd January 1967. (Milepost 92½)

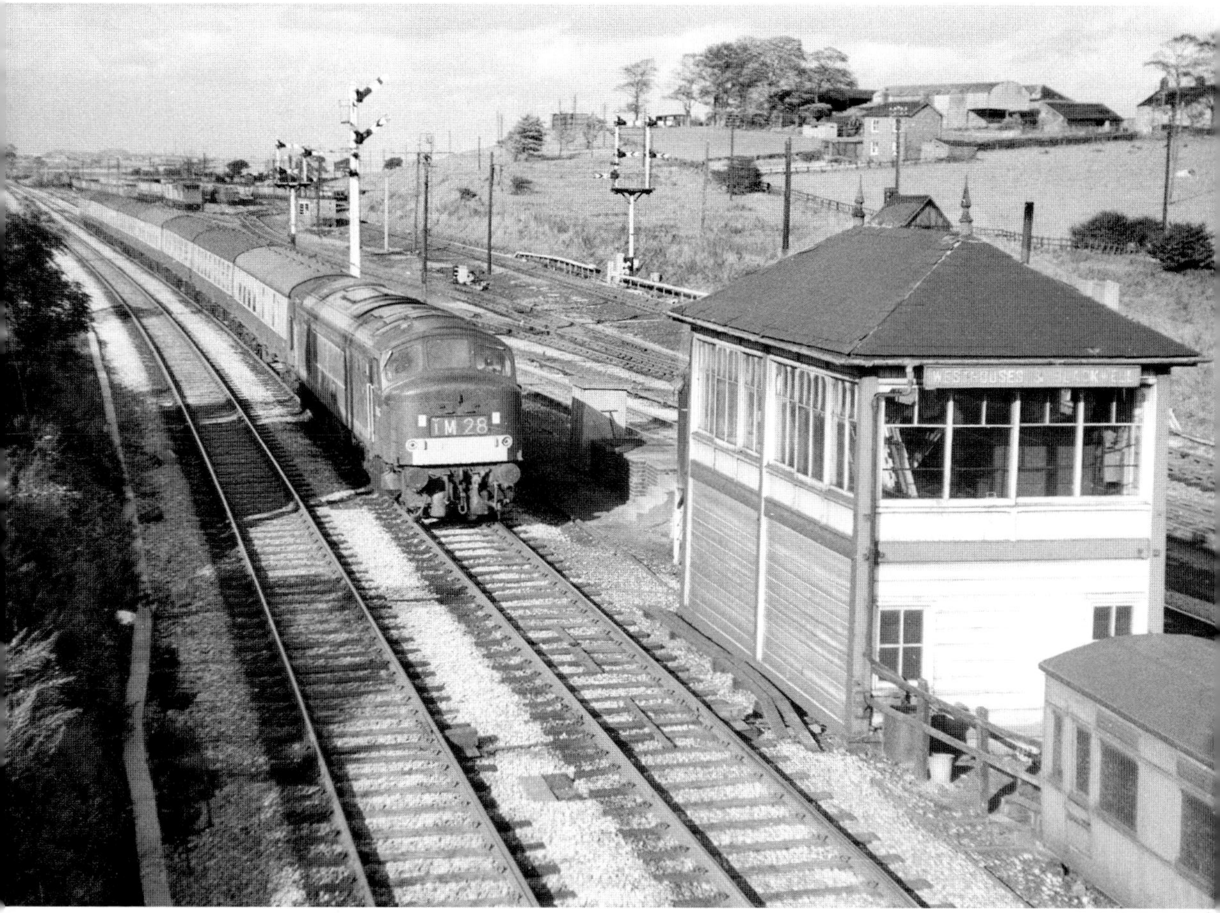

72. Westhouses & Blackwell signal box had 56 levers and it closed on 12th October 1969. In the background are Tibshelf Sidings, which served several collieries. The camera is on the road bridge in 1968. (A.F.Bullimore)

L. M. & S. R.
Issued subject to the conditions & regulations in the Co's Time Tables Books Bills & Notices.
Pye Bridge to
ALFRETON & S. NORMANTON
THIRD CLASS
3681(S) FARE -/4½
Alfreton&SN
2035

0296
2nd - SINGLE SINGLE - 2nd
Pye Bridge to
Pye Bridge Codnor Park & Ironville | Pye Bridge Codnor Park & Ironville
CODNOR PARK & IRONVILLE
(M) 0/2 Fare 0/2 (M)
For conditions see over For conditions see over
0296

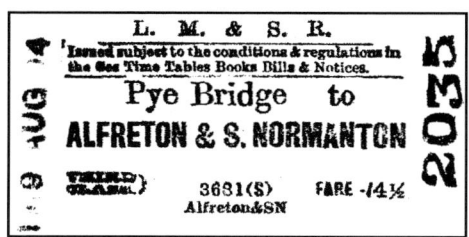

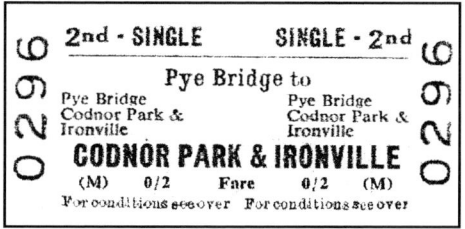

SOUTH OF DOE HILL

Tibshelf Sidings

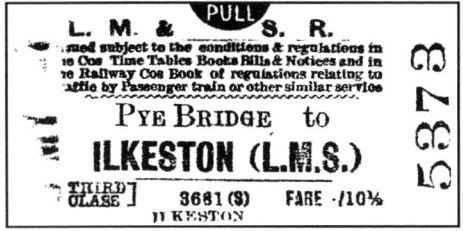

73. The full name of the box is evident. Its location is shown near the top of the sidings on the diagram under map XV. The frame contained 26 levers and closure came in February 1969. (M.J.Stretton coll.)

74. A photo from 13th August 1965 confirms the curves around the box and five modern electric lights, plus a water column, reaching for the sky. There appear to be oil drums in profusion. (R.J.Essery coll.)

Tibshelf Pits

75. These are Clay Cross Pits nos 3 & 4, also termed Tibshelf Pits. They were over one mile east of the main line and the branch to them was in use from 1894 to 1964. (Bevin Boys Assoc.)

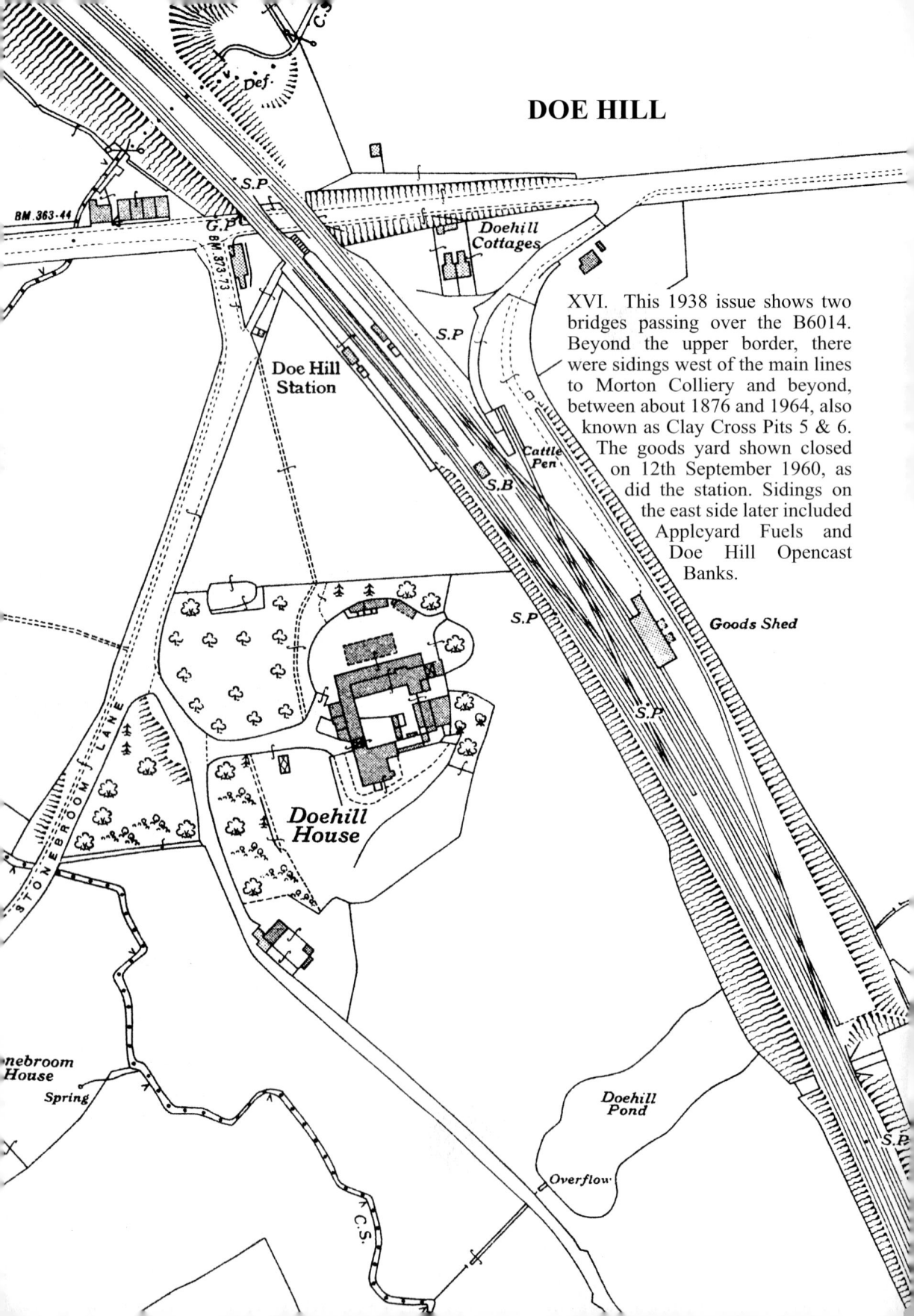

DOE HILL

Doehill Cottages

BM 363·44

BM 373·73

G.P.

Def.

S.P

S.P

Doe Hill Station

S.P

Cattle Pen

S.B

S.P

Goods Shed

S.P

STONEBROOM LANE

Doehill House

nebroom House

Spring

Doehill Pond

Overflow

C.S.

XVI. This 1938 issue shows two bridges passing over the B6014. Beyond the upper border, there were sidings west of the main lines to Morton Colliery and beyond, between about 1876 and 1964, also known as Clay Cross Pits 5 & 6. The goods yard shown closed on 12th September 1960, as did the station. Sidings on the east side later included Appleyard Fuels and Doe Hill Opencast Banks.

76.   The architectural style was different to those nearby. It came into use on 1st May 1862, with the opening of Codnor Park to Clay Cross. The nearby village of Morton housed 4144 in 1901, most being in the coal industry. (J.Alsop coll.)

77.   'Jubilee' class 4-6-0 no. 45622 *Nyasaland* is speeding through with the 12.15 Saturdays only St Pancras to Bradford express on 2nd April 1960. This signal box was in use from 1901 to 1969. (R.Humm coll.)

78. Two shafts and MR wagons are to be seen in this view termed Clay Cross '5 & 6 Pit'. They were west of the main line, near the village of Morton. (Bevin Boys Assoc.)

SOUTH OF CLAY CROSS

Iron Works

➜ XVII. This 1921 survey is at 6ins to 1 mile and has our route curving on the right. It continues on the next map and joins the main line from Derby at Clay Cross Junction at the top of this one. The Works is on the left and Collieries Nos 2 and 3 are to the right of it. Gas holders appeared under 'Coneygreen House' on the 1939 edition. Danesmoor Colliery was No. 7 and was nearer to Doe Hill, but on the east side of the main line. It can be found top left on map XIII, after picture 57. The railway pioneer George Stephenson discovered iron, coal and limestone strata here, while creating the tunnel lower left, in 1837. Thus, he started the industrial complex featured here. It became the Clay Company in 1852 and many name changes followed. In 1974, it was acquired by Ready Mixed Concrete of Australia.

> **For further details of the site,
> see map XVIII in our *Derby to Chesterfield* album.
> That map also contains the eastern end of the 2ft
> gauge Ashover Light Railway, which opened in 1925.
> The entire line is detailed in that volume.**

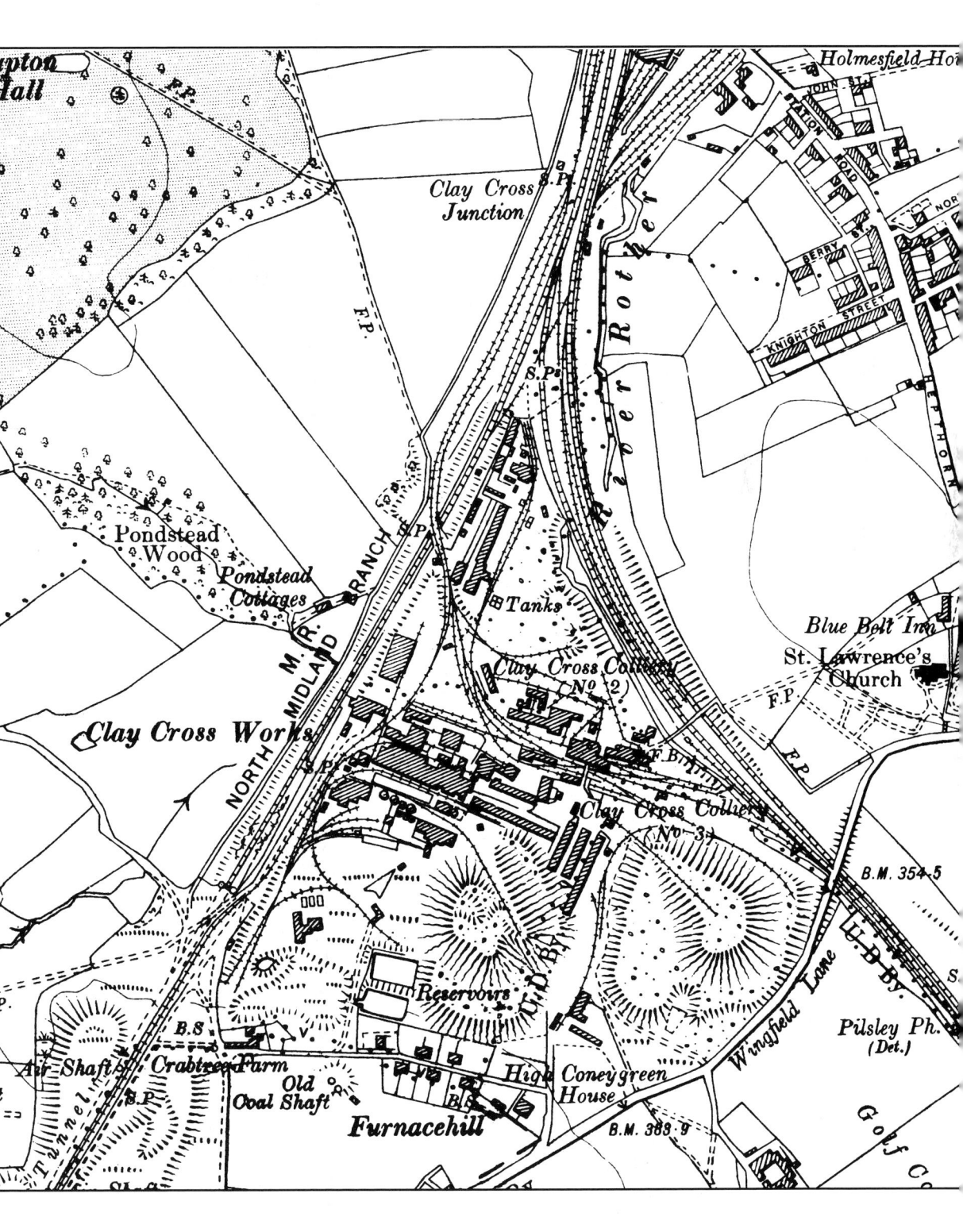

79. The workings known as 'Clay Cross Pits 2 & 3' were on the east side of the Iron Works, as stated, but the workings were very close to the main line tunnel. Near the lower right corner of the map was the colliery single line connection with the main line from Pye Bridge and also the bridge seen on the right. (Bevin Boys Assoc.)

80. This train is running from Chesterfield to Pye Bridge in September 1932. A parcels van separates the two compartment coaches behind the 0-4-4T. The points are near the right border of map XVII, where dots are in the middle of the River Rother, to indicate the parish boundary. (R.Humm coll.)

81.   We are in the Foundry on 10th June 1978. The shed is single road and brick-built. The sign reads, 'Danger. Beware of loco & wagons', but sadly this was no longer relevant as rail traffic had recently ceased and the two Ruston & Hornsby locos in the shed were for sale. No. 327970 of 1954 is visible. By the 1970s, most of the coke came overnight from Cwm, in South Wales. (A.J.Booth)

82.   Inside the foundry building on 5th July 1980 is specialist transport for the heavy iron pipes, which were exported worldwide. Four eight-wheeled units were built in-house circa 1969, 1971, 1973 and 1975, and these had, what they termed, a 'floating cable' above the locos, which was reeled in and out as the loco moved along. The fifth locomotive is the subject of the photo and was a conduit electric machine. There was a slot between the tracks and power was obtained by a connector, which went from the loco to a power rail under the conduit. This drove an electric motor that powered chain-drive final drive to one axle only. This loco worked on a single line of straight track inside a then-new pipe building. The gauge was 34ins, not 36 as in some reports. (A.J.Booth)

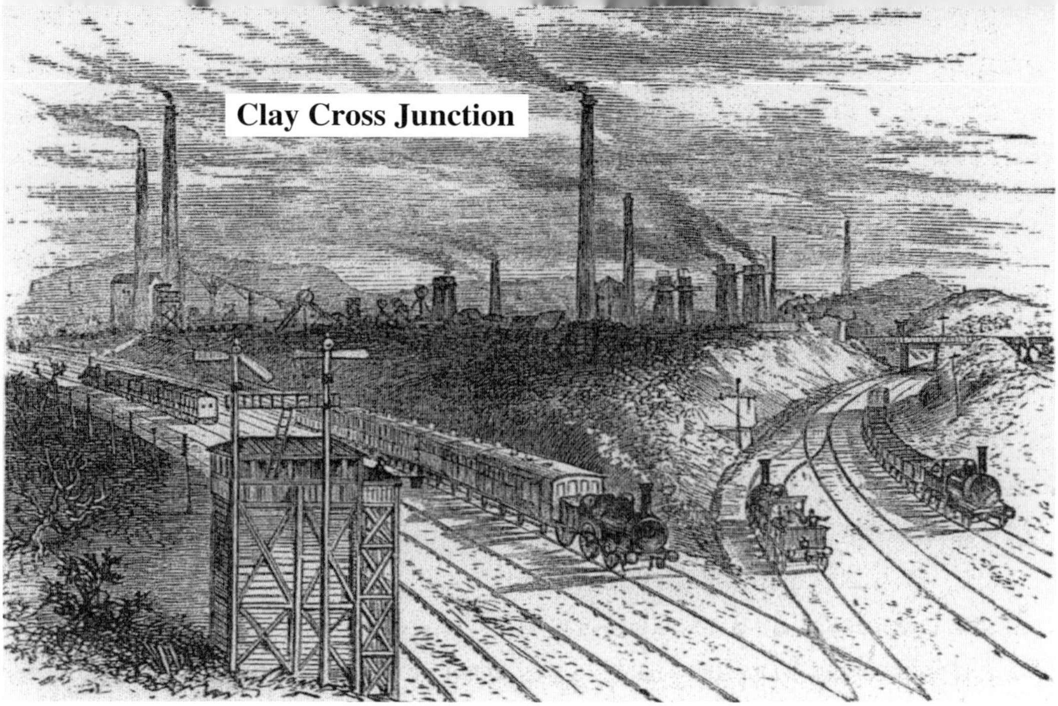

Clay Cross Junction

↑ 83. This southward view includes an early signal box, plus a flagmans hut on the left. The junction came into use in 1861 and the high level route on the right was usable from 1895 to 1963, but the bridge was earlier and was rebuilt. (R.Humm coll.)

→ 84. The Ashover Light Railway ceased to carry passengers on 19th September 1932, but minerals were hauled until September 1936, notably lime to help turn iron into steel. A tram body came to become a holiday home; it is near the left border of this picture, which is from 10th July 1976. No. 45142 has just left the line from Derby. (T.Heavyside)

↑ 85. Williamthorpe Colliery was about 1½ miles northeast of Clay Cross Junction and is seen in 1966. It was worked from November 1854 to March 1970. No. D8181 leads its companion, while track improvements are in progress.
(A.F.Bullimore)

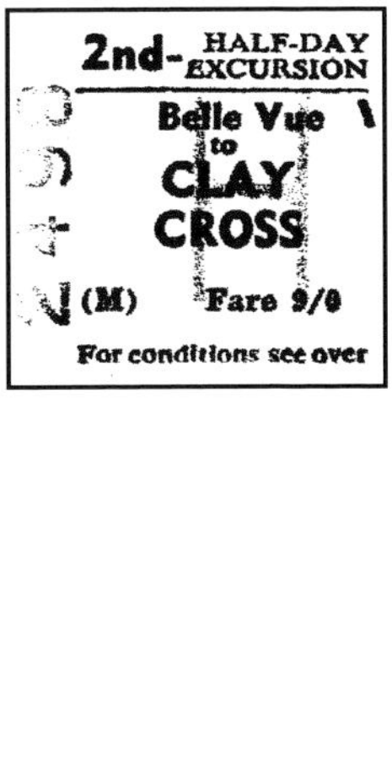

↑ 86. BR's original style lettering is shown on the tender of no. 44932, a class 5 4-6-0 on 28th April 1990. It was heading a railtour, which included Derby and Sheffield. It ran from and back to Marylebone and was called the 'Risborough Venturer'. (T.Heavyside)

→ 87. It is now 4th November 1995 and no. 60031 is hauling steel from Shelton, near Stoke to Teesside. The buffers in the previous picture have vanished and the skyline has changed, as it did quite frequently. (T.Heavyside)

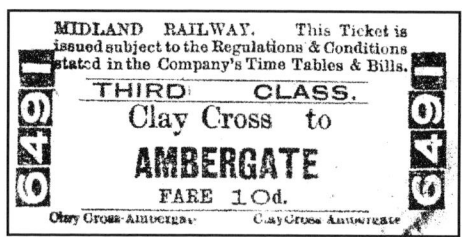

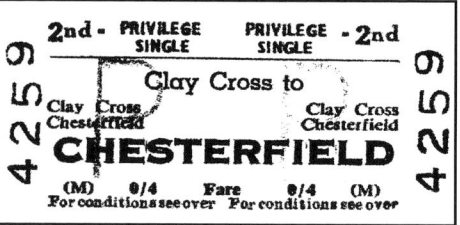

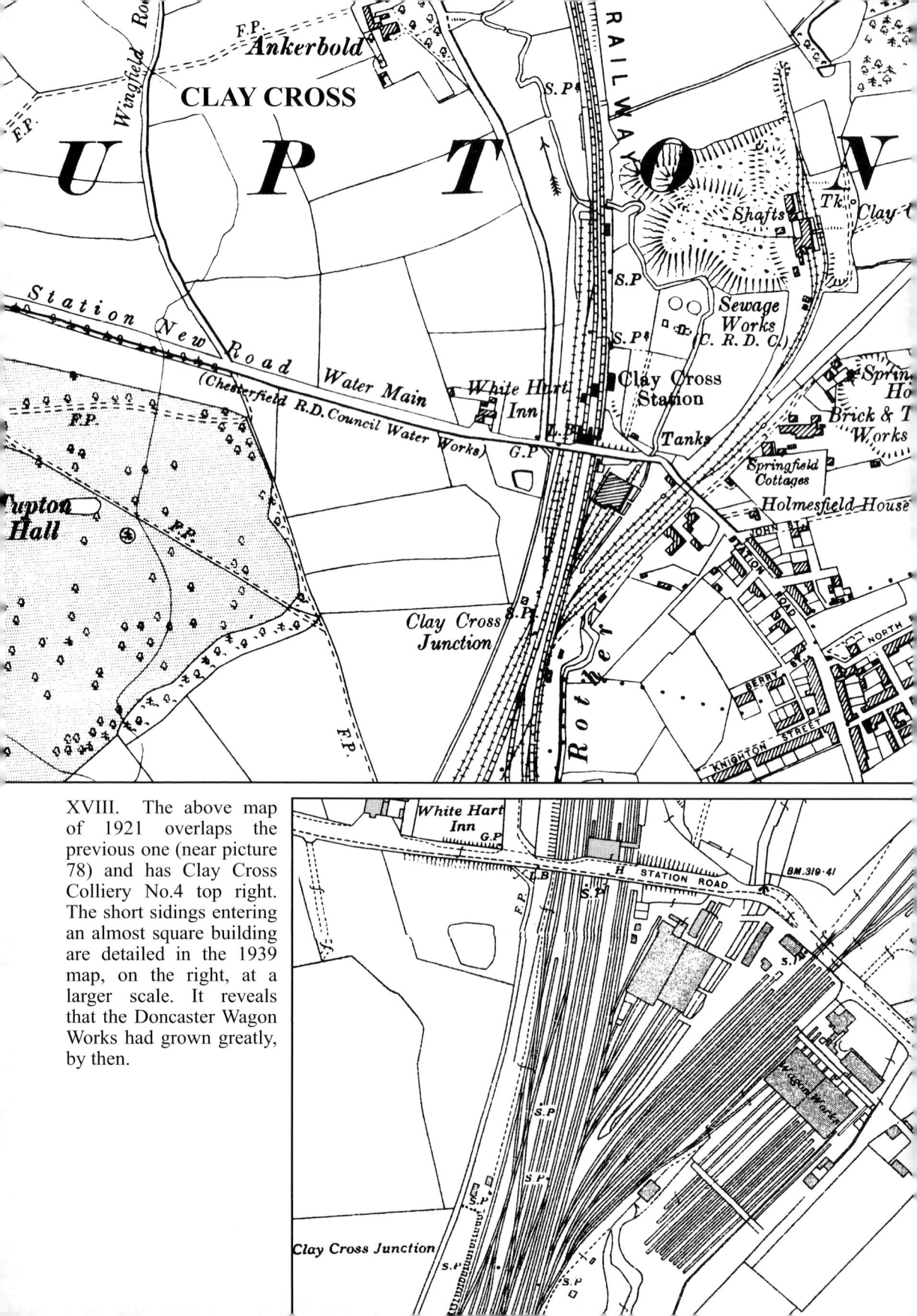

FP.
Ankerbold
CLAY CROSS
RAILWAY
S. P.
UPTON

Shafts Tk. Clay

S.P.

Sewage
Works
(C.R.D.C.)

Station New Road
Water Main
(Chesterfield R.D. Council Water Works)

S.P.
S.P.

White Hart
Inn
Clay Cross
Station

Spring
Ho

Brick & T
Works

G.P
Tanks

Springfield
Cottages

Holmesfield House

FP.

Tupton
Hall

JOHN ST.

STATION ROAD

FP.

Clay Cross
Junction
S.P.

Rother

NORTH

BERRY

KNIGHTON STREET

FP.

XVIII. The above map of 1921 overlaps the previous one (near picture 78) and has Clay Cross Colliery No.4 top right. The short sidings entering an almost square building are detailed in the 1939 map, on the right, at a larger scale. It reveals that the Doncaster Wagon Works had grown greatly, by then.

White Hart
Inn
G.P
STATION ROAD
BM.319·41

I.B
S.P.

S.P.

FP.
S.P.

Wagon Works

S.P.
S.P.

Clay Cross Junction
S.P.
S.P.

88.   A southward view has the four running lines to the left of the signal post and a tank engine standing adjacent to the goods yard. This was closed on 4th May 1964. There was another yard called Clay Cross Town. It was much closer to the town and some of the sidings on the left of map XVII were used. It closed on 7th October 1963. (LOSA)

89.   Here are the 'Collier Territorials' waiting to entrain for a fortnight's camp in the Peak District. The 'Getters', noted in the inscription below, are the actual people who dig the coal; it was an ancient mining term. No. 4 Colliery is in the background. Sadly, the date was not recorded. (J.Alsop coll.)

No. 110.]   [See Nos. 109 & 114.

COLLIER-TERRITORIALS.
Getters of the renowned "C.X.C. Gold Medal" Coal entraining at Clay Cross Station for the Peak of Derbyshire for a fortnight's camp. No. 4 Pit in the background.

90. The first station was of Italianate style and lasted from its opening on 6th April 1841 until about 1861, when the main line was quadrupled. This view is under the booking hall in October 1951. (R.Humm coll.)

91. The station closed on 2nd January 1967. Another 1951 shot includes all four platforms and also the North Junction Box. It is on the map, below the 'O' of UPTON. It had 56 levers and was in use from 1902 to 1969. (R.Humm coll.)

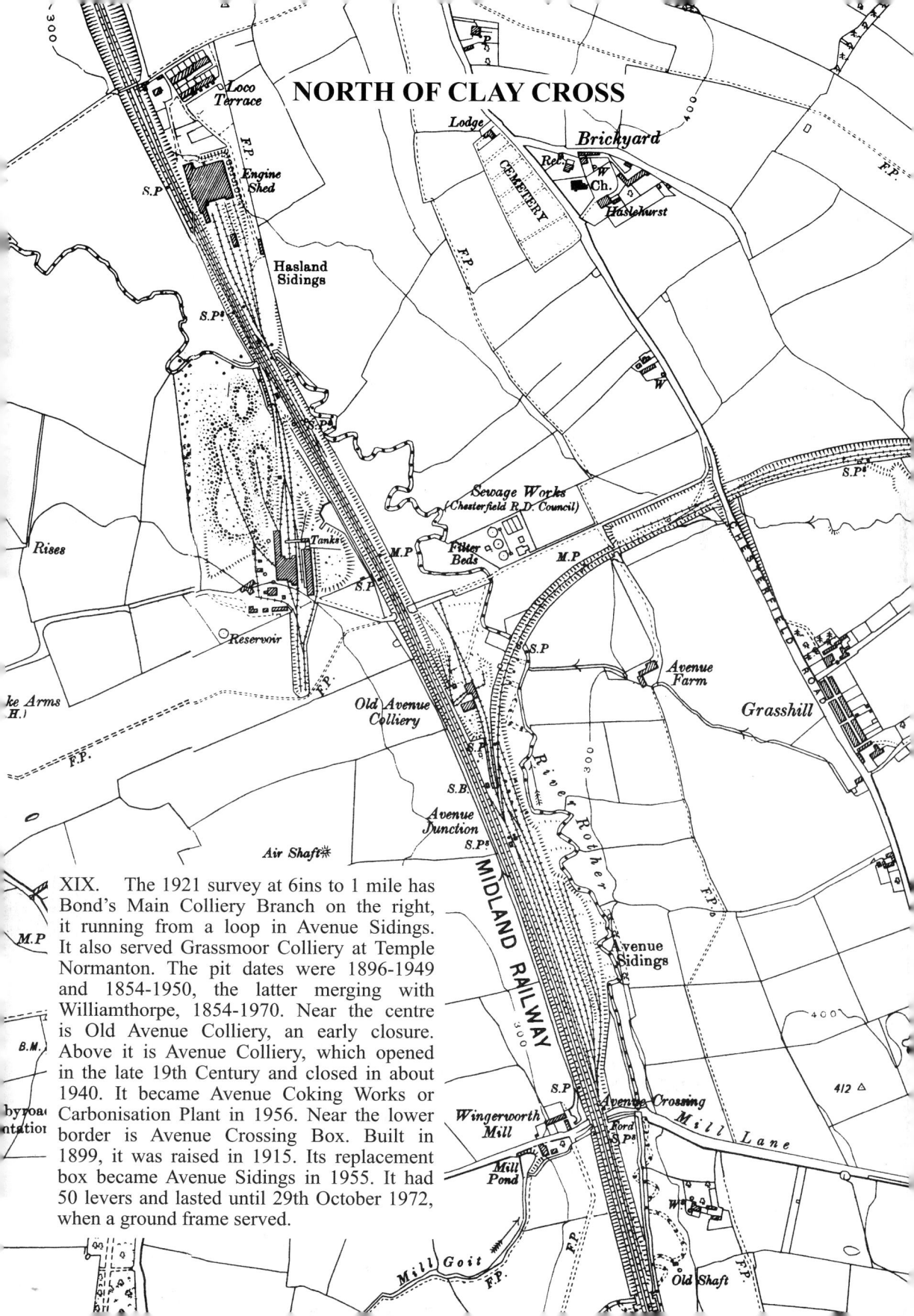

XIX.   The 1921 survey at 6ins to 1 mile has Bond's Main Colliery Branch on the right, it running from a loop in Avenue Sidings. It also served Grassmoor Colliery at Temple Normanton. The pit dates were 1896-1949 and 1854-1950, the latter merging with Williamthorpe, 1854-1970. Near the centre is Old Avenue Colliery, an early closure. Above it is Avenue Colliery, which opened in the late 19th Century and closed in about 1940. It became Avenue Coking Works or Carbonisation Plant in 1956. Near the lower border is Avenue Crossing Box. Built in 1899, it was raised in 1915. Its replacement box became Avenue Sidings in 1955. It had 50 levers and lasted until 29th October 1972, when a ground frame served.

↑ 92. Although not sharp, this image confirms the extent of the sidings in steam days. The branch feeding them would be on the far-right and in the left background is evidence of the Carbonisation Plant, clearer in the next view. On the site had been Wingerworth Colliery until 1950. (W.Taylor coll.)

→ 93. No. 47086 is heading an up passenger service on 10th July 1976. Beyond the train is a recent bridge added to link the Exchange Sidings with the Carbonisation Plant, where smokeless fuels were being produced in increasing quantities. It operated from 1956 to 1992 and produced much domestic quality coke, known as Sunbrite. (T.Heavyside)

↗ 94. Yellow four-wheeled diesel shunters have each brought in loaded coal trains, for onward haulage by larger locomotives. Seen here are two Thomas Hill 'Vanguard' 0-4-0 diesel-hydraulics, nos 6 and 7, built in 1968 and 1970 respectively and transferred to Avenue in 1978. They were built in Rotherham. (Colour-Rail.com)

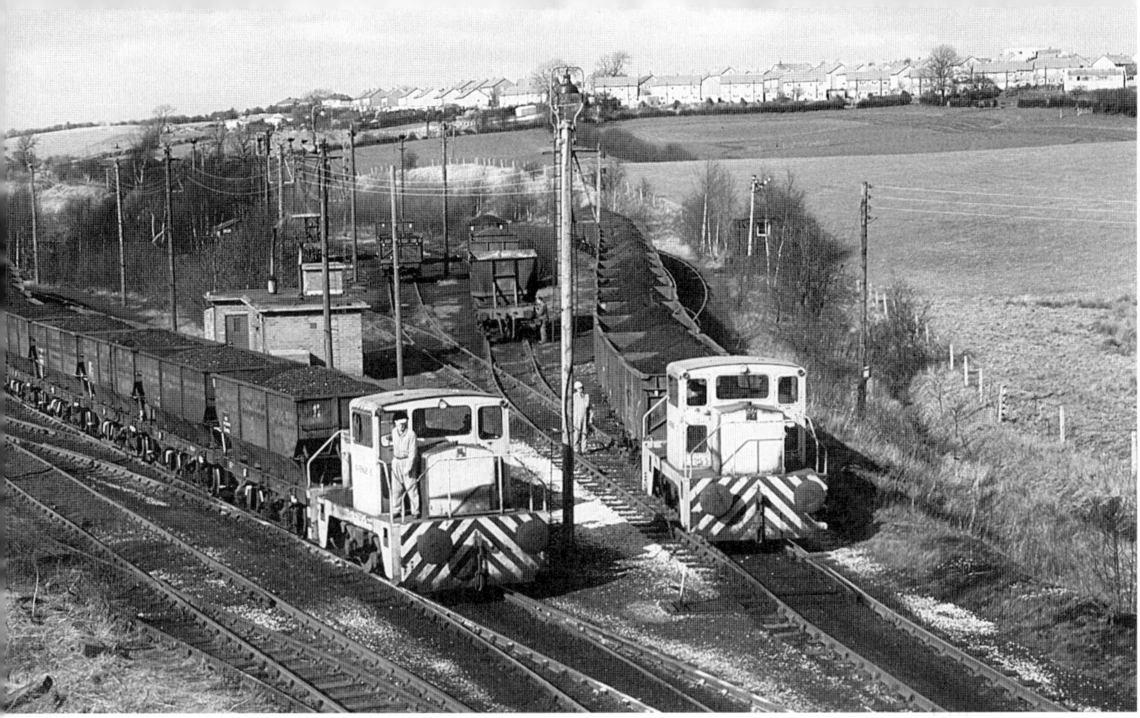

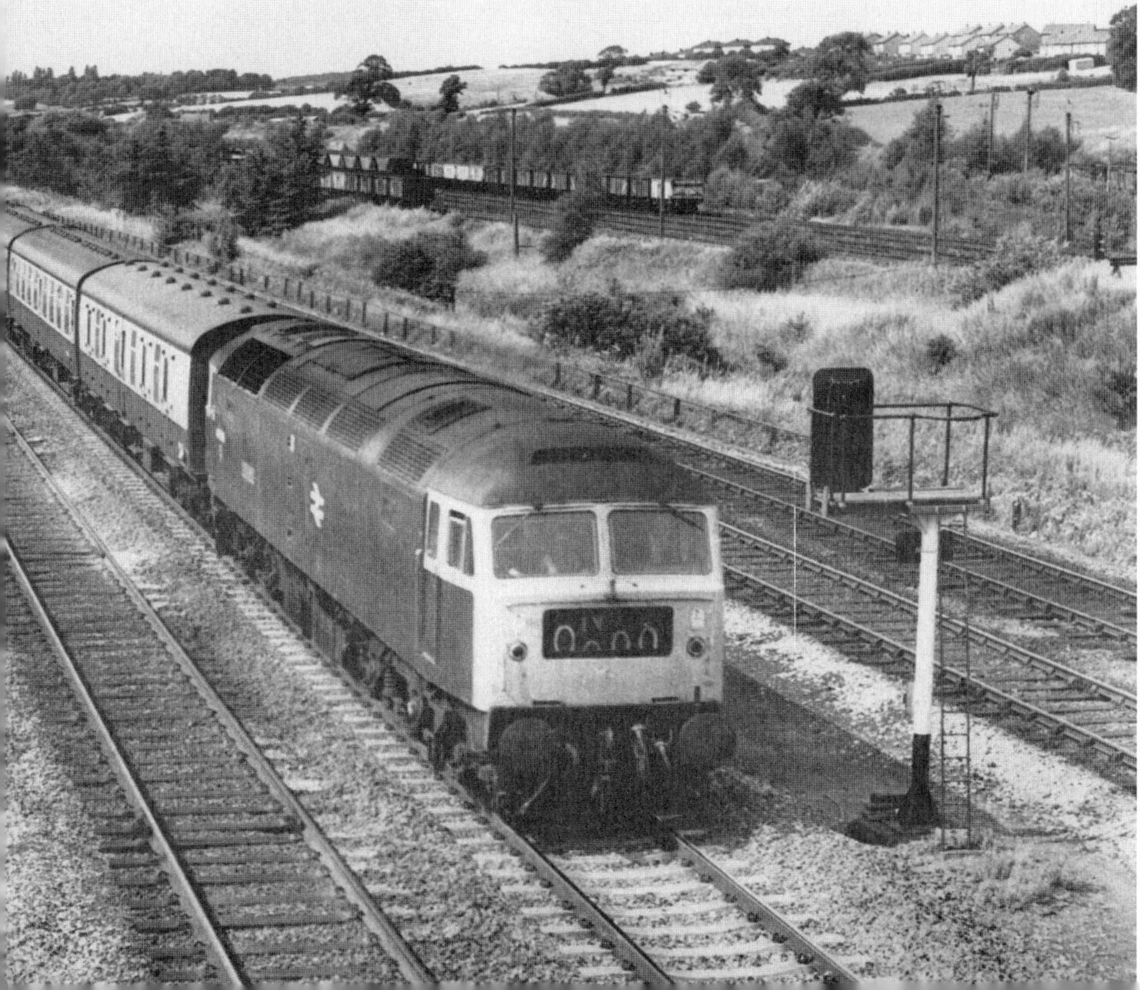

95. Here are nos 20010 and 20141 in Railfreight red-stripe livery departing from Avenue Sidings with the network coal service to Toton on 6th April 1988 at 17.55. This area is now a nature reserve and country park. Only the road bridge over the main line remains in place. (R.Geach)

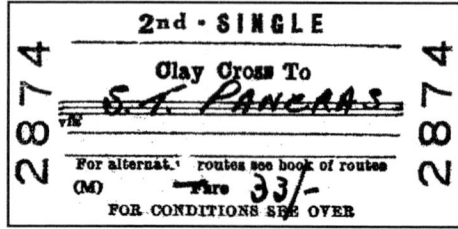

2nd · SINGLE
Clay Cross To
S.T. PANCRAS
For alternat.' routes see book of routes
(M) Fare 33/-
FOR CONDITIONS SEE OVER
2874

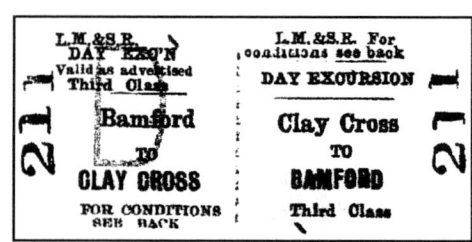

L.M.&S.R.
DAY REQ'N
Valid as advertised
Third Class
Bamford
TO
CLAY CROSS
FOR CONDITIONS
SEE BACK

L.M.&S.R. For
conditions see back
DAY EXCURSION
Clay Cross
TO
BAMFORD
Third Class
21

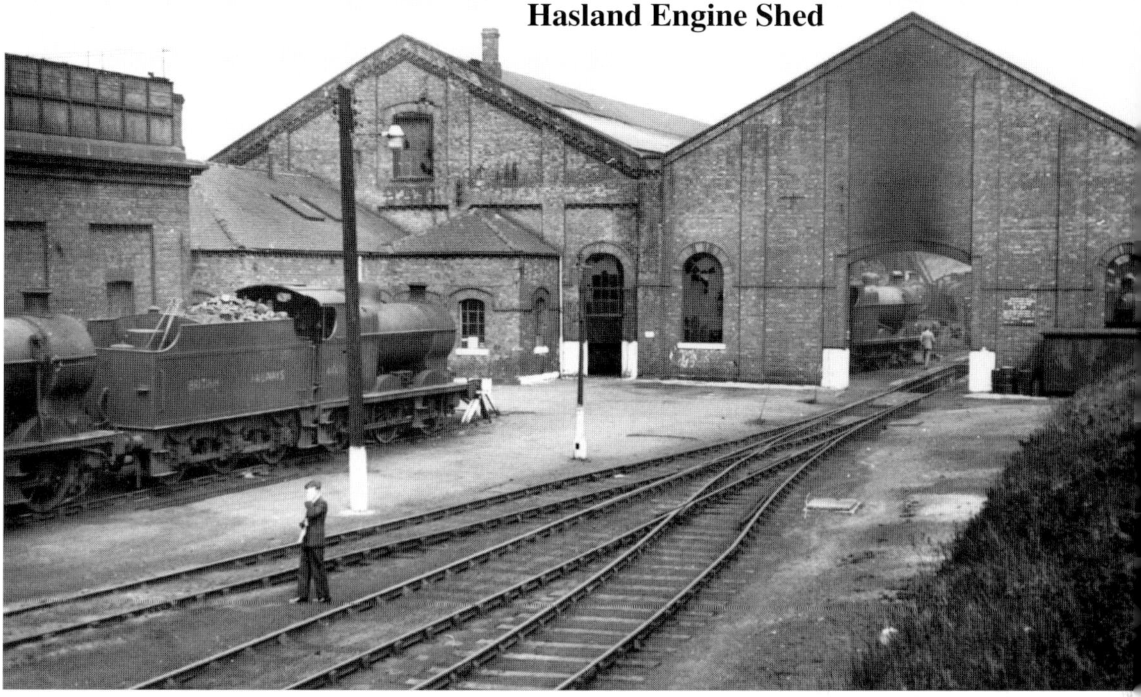

Hasland Engine Shed

96. The shed was opened in 1861 and was almost two miles from Chesterfield station. There were signal boxes nearby; one at Horns Bridge in 1963-69 and one at Hollis Lane in 1899-1966. This view is from August 1954 and shows the only line to enter the building, albeit the part that had lost its roof. (R.Humm coll.)

97. Upon entering, there was immediate access to the turntable, from which 24 sidings radiated. An old roof support is included, but no details of the engines survive. There were 49 allocated here in 1950, of which 10 were the massive 2-6-6-2T Beyer Garratts. (Colour-Rail.com)

98.   The shed code was 18C from 1948 to 1963 and then 16H until closure in 1964. This view is from 23rd March 1958; there were only 18 residents left by 1959. The hose on the right supplied power to turn the turntable, when it was connected to the vacuum brake pipe between an engine's buffers. (Colour-Rail.com)

Hasland

99.   Levers numbered 55 and closure came on 12th October 1969 for Hasland Sidings box. It is seen in 1968, with the colliery waste tip behind. (A.F.Bullimore)

SOUTH OF CHESTERFIELD
Bank Close

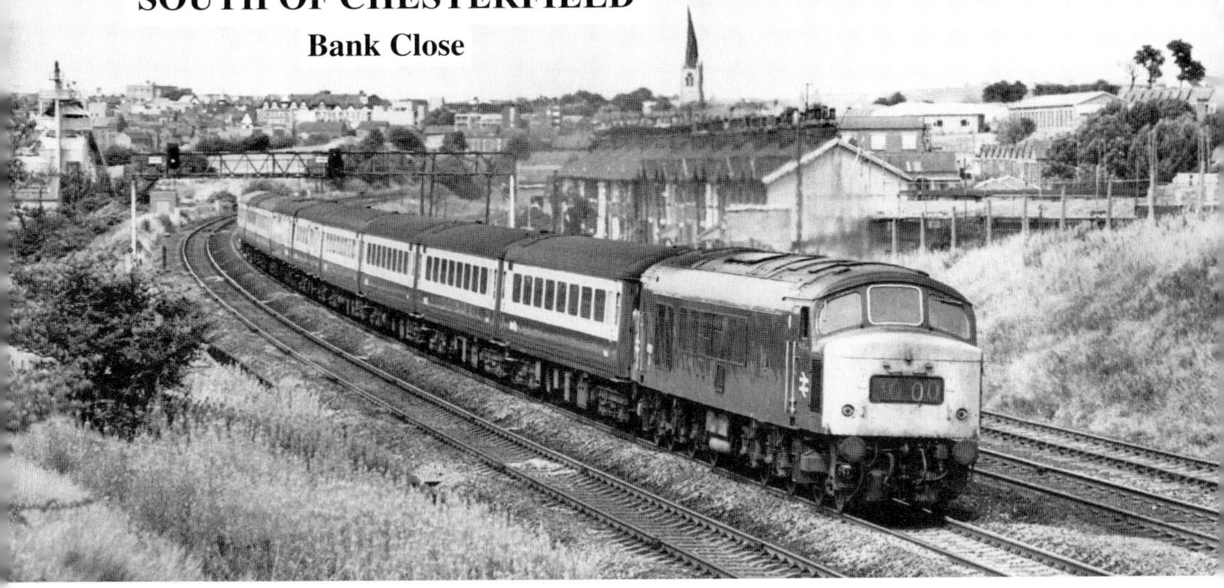

100. No. 45121 departs south on 10th July 1976. The location is about one mile south of the station, which is to the right of the famous crooked spire on the parish church. (T.Heavyside)

101. Accelerating away on 16th September 2000 is DMU no. 170509. This sub-class of Turbostar units was built by Adtranz in Derby in 1999-2000. The church now seems more inspiring. (R.J.Stewart-Smith)

102. No. 66569 is seen on 25th June 2012. It was one of a group of low emission locos operated by Freightliner at that time. The operator was Heavy Haul, which was the bulk freight division of Freightliner. (R.J.Stewart-Smith)

➜ XX. Between this map and the previous one there is a gap of almost a mile. Both are 1921 surveys at 6ins to 1 mile. Between them were four sidings on the west side shown near the disused Broad Oaks Furnaces and, on the east side, one for Storforth Lane Brick Works. The adjacent village was Birdholme. We terminate our trip at the MR station, on the right of this map. To the left of it is the GCR one, together with its long tunnel. These were in use from 1893 to 1963. The terminus near the left border received trains from Lincoln and was called Market Place. It was open from 1897 to 1957 and was a GCR line in 1907-23. Spital Mills were named after the nearby hospital. The MR Gas Works had been lower centre; a single siding is still shown on the bank side. The lower line on the left border ran to the MR Brampton Road Goods depot, plus several private sidings, including one for the Electricity Works.

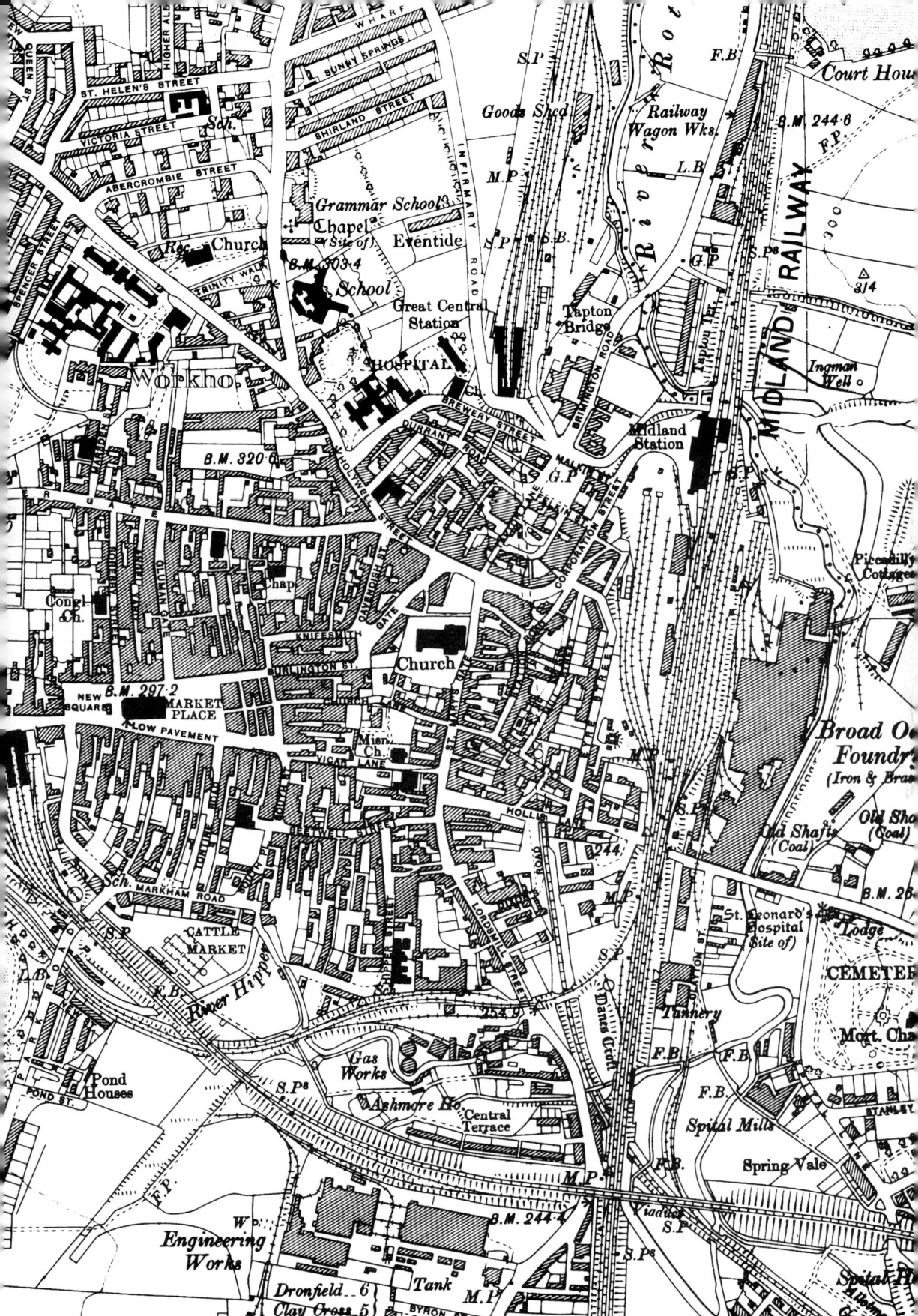

103. MR 4-4-0 no. 553 is accelerating, having run under part of the branch to the GCR terminus. The posts on the right are a reminder that the main railways had offered the first public telegram and telephone services. (R.M.Casserley coll.)

Bradshaw hotel advertisements, 1905.

104. The curved track running under the main line on the last map was termed the GCR Loop and is seen with the Viaduct, marked as such. A class 8F 2-8-0 is centre-stage. These were introduced in 1935. On the right is South Box. (J.Suter coll.)

105. This view of The Loop is from a main line train in about 1960. Some of the many bridges can be found on the last map. The church spire had become distorted from about 1360, as detailed in our *Derby to Chesterfield* album. (R.J.Essery coll.)

➡ 106.   This view is from October 1957. The lower bridge carries the main lines and is named Horns Bridge. The upper one carried goods traffic to and from Brampton Depot until 4th March 1957. (J.Suter coll.)

⬇ 107.   The results of demolition work on the former GCR structure are seen from a down main line train on 11th June 1965. The remaining viaduct span was over Hasland Road. There was another one west of the main line. The new Horns Bridge box was of Eastern Region pattern and replaced the MR one, which had 35 levers and was on the opposite side of the tracks. It was in use from 1892 to 1963, when the one seen was opened. This lasted until 1969. (H.C.Casserley)

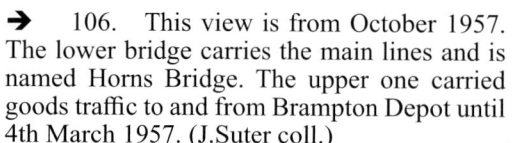

M. & S. R.

Issued subject to the conditions & regulations in the Coy Time Tables Books Bills & Notices and in the Railway Coy Book of regulations relating to traffic by Passenger train or other similar service

Chesterfield to

CLAY CROSS

THIRD CLASS   3236(S)   FARE -/7
             Clay Cross

2/ 85 3   00 00 30

MIDLAND RAILWAY. This Ticket is issued subject to the Regulations & Conditions stated in the Company's Time Tables & Bills.

FIRST CLASS.   FIRST CLASS.
AVAILABLE ON DAY OF ISSUE ONLY.

CHESTERFIELD to

DERBY (MID)

FARE 3s. 2d.   FARE 3s. 2d.
Ches'field-Derby   Ches'field Derby

9211   9211

CHESTERFIELD

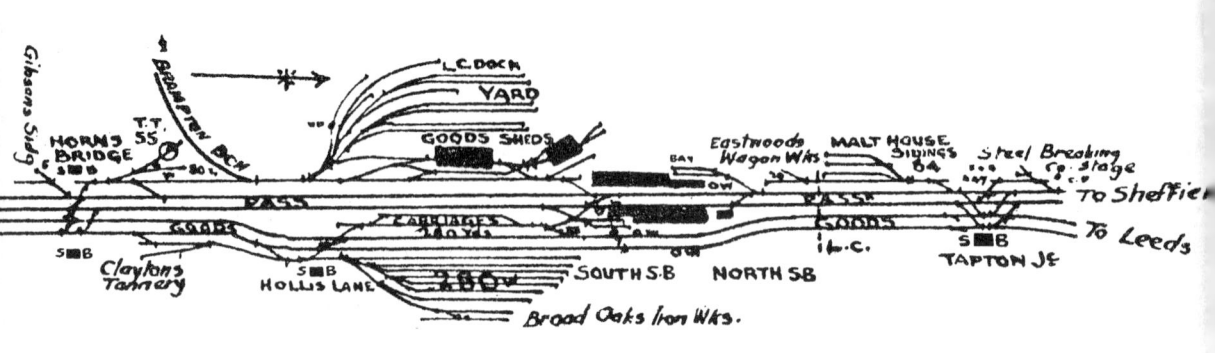

XXI. The MR diagram was undated, but seems to show the layout at its optimum. The figure 280 refers to the yard capacity in wagons.

108. To the left of the bridge over the River Rother is the Midland Station and its goods shed. The multi-storey building is Station Hotel. Meadows abound. The unfortunate spire suffered a severe fire on 21st March 1861, due to lightning, which struck a gas lighting pipe. (J.Alsop coll.)

109. A fine postcard presents the prospective passenger's perspective in the days when horses had to be fed between trips. BR still employed 26,240 for parcel traffic in 1948. The figures were 457 in 1958 and 18 in 1959. The first station was open from 11th May 1840 until 2nd May 1870 and was about 100 yards south of this one, which lasted until 1963. (LOSA)

110. This early card has the station approach road and the adjacent river on the right. Overseeing them is the Station Hotel, well situated for railway observers to enjoy the view. St Mary and All Saints is the largest church in the county and is listed Grade I. (LOSA)

111. The main building carries an enamelled board promoting the MIDLAND HOTEL. Such large businesses would receive milk in churns of the type in the foreground. Milk tankers became common in trains in the 1930s. (LOSA)

112. Seen on 10th June 1950 with a down goods train is class 3F 0-6-0 no. 43299, a type dating from 1885. This is the 1915 North Box. It closed on 25th March 1973. South Box was working from 1915 until 12th October 1969. There was a subway for healthy passengers to use. (Bentley coll.)

113. The suffix can be seen again on a BR board. It was in use this time from 18th June 1951 to 7th September 1964. Parcels abound in an era when there was a LADIES WAITING ROOM still. Some trains had dedicated compartments also. (LOSA)

114. The well-styled second station lasted until 1965. The roof of the third building is partially visible on the right. It was rather featureless and lasted only until 1996. The suffix seen on the left was changed to ST MARY'S from 25th September 1950 to 18th June 1951. This was half the name of the nearby church. (LOSA)

↑ 115. Ex-WD 2-8-0 no. 90220 is on the down goods line with the 11.20 Ashwell to Frodingham service on 8th August 1964. Wagon load traffic ended in 1984; only complete trains were acceptable thereafter. Hollis Lane signal box was near the rear of the train and it only controlled the goods line. It was in use from 1899 to 1966. Hollis Lane can be found on the last map. (E.Wilmshurst)

↗ 116.   It is 5th July 1972 and it is clear that the platform awnings were retained during the replacement of the main buildings. The bay platforms were often used for parcel traffic, as seen. (H.C.Casserley)

→ 117. No. 6773 is heading an up passenger train on 15th July 1972. No. 16 is on the right. The former was an English Electric Type 3 Co-Co and on the right is a Type 4 'Peak'. (T.Heavyside)

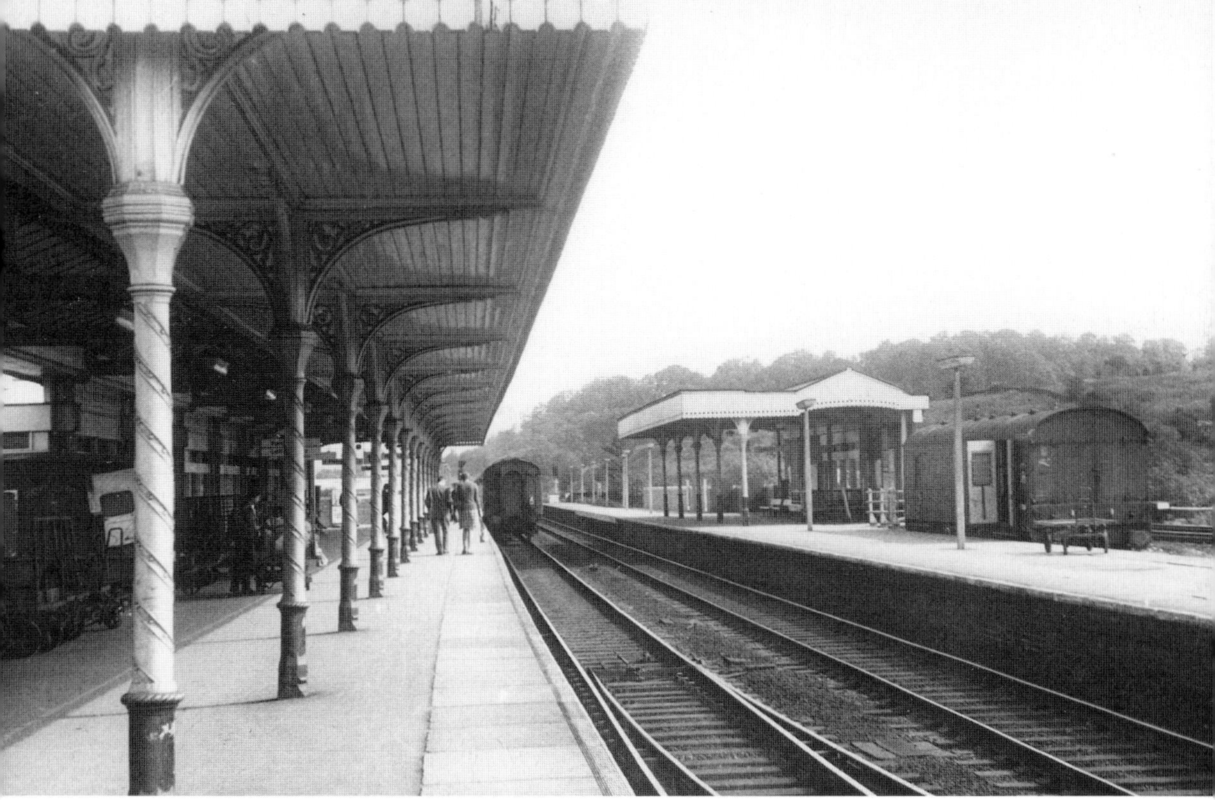

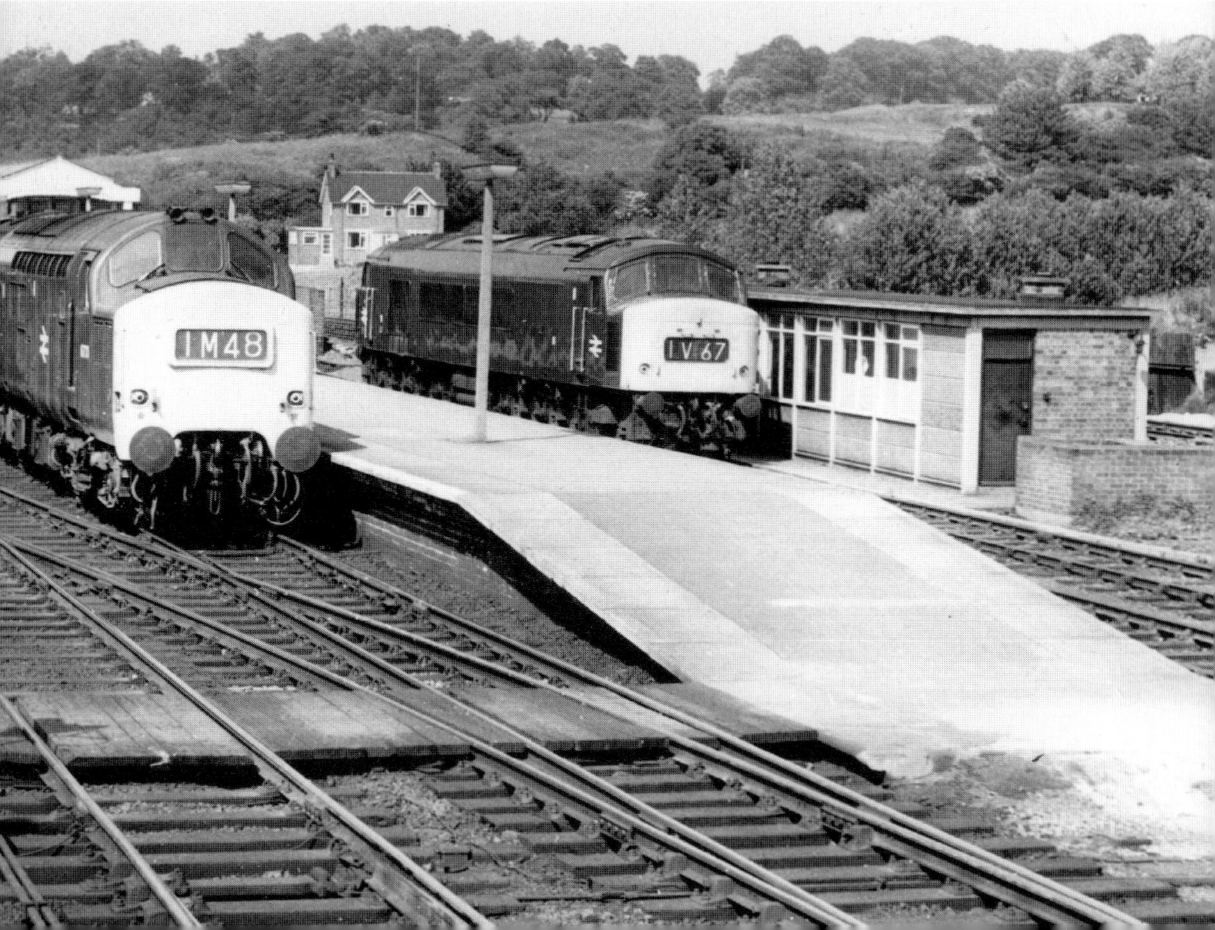
1M48
1V67

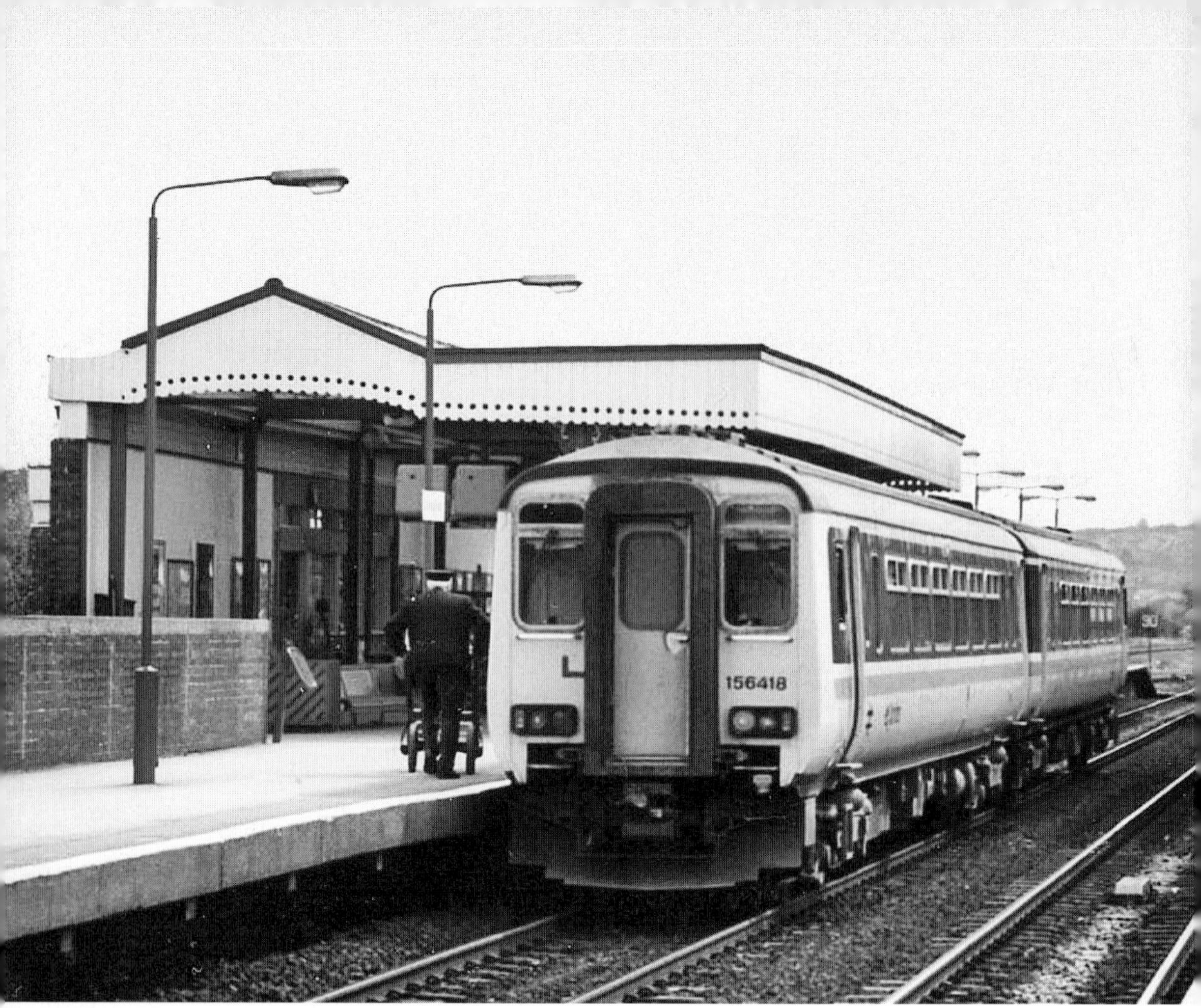
156418

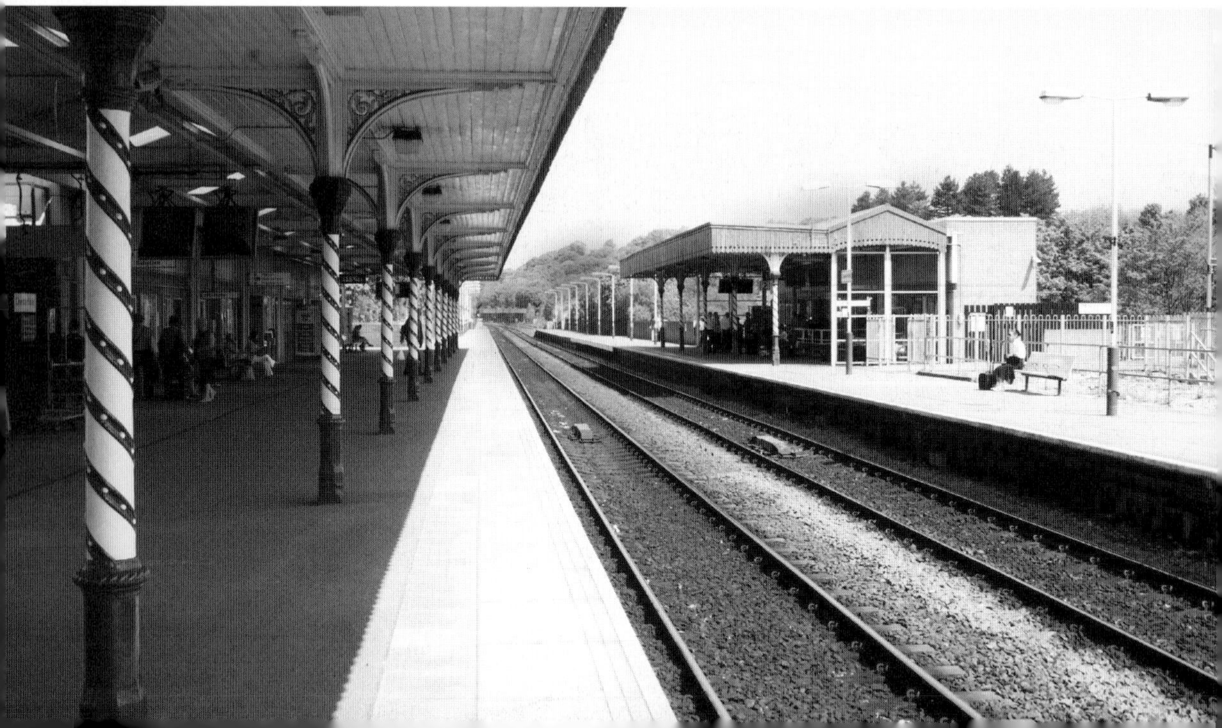

← 118. DMU no. 156418 waits to depart for Nottingham on 8th May 1991, while an HST arrives. By 2000, the two disused goods sheds were the only historic buildings still standing in this vicinity. The goods yard's public traffic ended on 15th January 1964. (P.Jones)

↖ 119. Platform 3 is bidirectional and was opened in July 2010. From May 2015, it was used by some services on the Leeds-Nottingham and Liverpool-Norwich routes at peak periods and during engineering works to reduce dependence on replacement bus services. It is located on the down slow line, backing on to Platform 2, and is long enough to accommodate a 10-car train. Platform 3 had existed in previous decades, although it was a bay platform. It can be glimpsed in pictures 114 and 115. The right lamp is provided for it in this fine view, which is from 23rd May 2012. In the next financial year, there were 1.5m passengers using the station. (Colour-Rail.com)

↓ 120. There was another total rebuild of the main building in 1996, its facade offering generous natural lighting thereafter. The bronze statue (centre, in this image from 2015) is of George Stephenson (1781-1848) and in his hand is a model of his *Locomotion No. 1*. The position of the subway is evident in the previous picture. (Colour-Rail.com)

EVOLVING THE
ULTIMATE RAIL ENCYCLOPEDIA
INTERNATIONAL

Easebourne Midhurst GU29 9AZ. Tel:01730 813169

A-978 0 906520 B- 978 1 873793 C- 978 1 901706 D-978 1 904474
E - 978 1 906008 F - 978 1 908174 G - 978 1 910356

Our RAILWAY titles are listed below. Please check availability by looking at our website **www.middletonpress.co.uk**, telephoning us or by requesting a Brochure which includes our LATEST RAILWAY TITLES also our TRAMWAY, TROLLEYBUS, MILITARY and COASTAL series.

email:info@middletonpress.co.uk